MASTERING
BASIC
VOCABULARY

MASTERING BASIC VOCABULARY

WILLIAM STRONG
Utah State University

RANDOM HOUSE NEW YORK

First Edition
987654321
Copyright © 1984 by Random House, Inc.

Library of Congress Cataloging in Publication Data
Strong, William, 1940–
    Mastering basic vocabulary.

    (Sentence combining in action)
    Includes index.
    1. Vocabulary.   2. English language—Sentences—
Problems, exercises, etc.   I. Title.   II. Series:
Strong, William, 1940–   . Sentence combining in
action.
PE1449.S84   1983   428.1   83-16003
ISBN 0-394-33615-1

Manufactured in the United States of America

Text Design by: Dana Kasarsky Design
Illustrations by: Jackie Merritt

for Ken Fleming

A NOTE TO INSTRUCTORS

This book aims to help students master basic vocabulary—a variety of frequently confused words—and simultaneously improve basic sentence skills.

Students should not write in the text.

The reasons for *not* writing in the book are both pedagogical and practical: (1) Students learn to write complete sentences by *writing* them, not by "filling in the blanks"; (2) this text can be used by many students if it has not been written in.

The "closure cues" provided in the WRITE and CHECK parts of each sentence combining exercise are "mental starters"—hints for putting sentences together. They assist students with either oral/choral practice or sentence-level writing in their own notebooks.

A ten-item Mastery Quiz is found at the end of each section of exercises. Like the WRITE and CHECK practice, quiz items should be written out as complete sentences and corrected.

A double-entry index is included so that students needing help with particular words can find the location of appropriate exercises. The exercise sequences are arranged in order of slowly increasing difficulty.

An Instructor's Manual for the *Sentence Combining in Action* series is available upon request from the College Department at Random House, 201 East 50th Street, New York, NY 10022. This manual contains the answer key for all Mastery Quizzes in this text.

ACKNOWLEDGMENTS

On a gray, rainy October afternoon in 1978—while driving mind-numbing I-80 eastward across Nebraska and Iowa—I got so deeply into the gymnastics of creating basic vocabulary exercises that I made a full circle around Davenport, Iowa and found myself heading *west* on the road I had just traveled. Later, on the same sabbatical trip, it was Bill Horst in Virginia who saw the potential of such exercises for teaching sentence construction and spelling/vocabulary skills simultaneously.

Special thanks go to the reviewers of the manuscript for their insightful comments and suggestions: Hugh Burns, United States Air Force Academy; Barbara Gray, Polytechnic Institute of New York; Robert Plec, Oakland Community College; and Richard Tracey, Cerritos Community College. I also want to acknowledge Will Pitkin, William E. Smith, and my colleagues in Secondary Education at Utah State University for their continuing support.

Finally, I am grateful to Steve Pensinger and Steve Young at Random House for their hard work on the *Sentence Combining in Action* series and to my family for shepherding me through it.

CONTENTS

AN INTRODUCTION TO SENTENCE COMBINING   1

MASTERING VOCABULARY THROUGH SENTENCE
COMBINING   5

SEQUENCE A EXERCISES   21
   MASTERY QUIZ A   24

SEQUENCE B EXERCISES   25
   MASTERY QUIZ B   28

SEQUENCE C EXERCISES   29
   MASTERY QUIZ C   32

SEQUENCE D EXERCISES   33
   MASTERY QUIZ D   37

SEQUENCE E EXERCISES   38
   MASTERY QUIZ E   41

SEQUENCE F EXERCISES   42
   MASTERY QUIZ F   46

SEQUENCE G EXERCISES   47
   MASTERY QUIZ G   50

SEQUENCE H EXERCISES   51
   MASTERY QUIZ H   54

SEQUENCE I EXERCISES   55
   MASTERY QUIZ I   59

SEQUENCE J EXERCISES   60
   MASTERY QUIZ J   63

SEQUENCE K EXERCISES   64
   MASTERY QUIZ K   68

SEQUENCE L EXERCISES   69
   MASTERY QUIZ L   73

SEQUENCE M EXERCISES   74
   MASTERY QUIZ M   78

SEQUENCE N EXERCISES   79
   MASTERY QUIZ N   83

SEQUENCE O EXERCISES   84
   MASTERY QUIZ O   88

SEQUENCE P EXERCISES   89
   MASTERY QUIZ P   93

SEQUENCE Q EXERCISES   94
MASTERY QUIZ Q   97

SEQUENCE R EXERCISES   99
MASTERY QUIZ R   104

SEQUENCE S EXERCISES   105
MASTERY QUIZ S   109

SEQUENCE T EXERCISES   110
MASTERY QUIZ T   114

SEQUENCE U EXERCISES   115
MASTERY QUIZ U   119

SEQUENCE V EXERCISES   120

MASTERY QUIZ V   124

SEQUENCE W EXERCISES   126
MASTERY QUIZ W   130

SEQUENCE X EXERCISES   131
MASTERY QUIZ X   135

SEQUENCE Y EXERCISES   137
MASTERY QUIZ Y   141

SEQUENCE Z EXERCISES   143
MASTERY QUIZ Z   148

INDEX   251

MASTERING BASIC VOCABULARY

AN INTRO-
DUCTION
TO
SENTENCE
COMBINING

Ever since the late 1960s and early 1970s, a quiet revolution in the way writing is taught has been gaining momentum. The emphasis has shifted from *taking sentences apart*—the "grammar approach"—to *putting sentences together*. This new approach is called *sentence combining*—or SC, for short.

SC makes use of what a person already knows about how words go together. Its purpose, simply stated, is to improve a person's skill in constructing clear, correct English sentences. To improve basic writing skills, groups of short, choppy sentences are rewritten into more mature and interesting prose.

SC exercises come in many varieties and formats. What all exercises have in common, however, is the challenge to put given meanings (short sentences) into new, expanded sentence forms called *writeouts*. It's the *practice* in combining—orally "rehearsing" possible writeouts, changing word endings or connecting words, reading and rewriting for clarity—that makes the approach so powerful.

Over the years a variety of *cues*, or signals, have been developed for SC exercises. These structured hints nudge a person toward constructing sentences in predetermined ways.

The structured approach used here presents cues in the form of partially completed writeouts. The task is to fill in the blanks mentally with meanings from SC exercises. Structured exercises provide enough framework to guide the writer toward making clear and interesting sentences, using a wide repertoire of structures characteristic of standard written English.

In *Mastering Basic Vocabulary,* structured exercises reinforce the learning of spelling and vocabulary. Following definitions and sentences containing commonly misspelled and misused words, structured exercises are presented to provide practice using these words in *context*. Mental processing, not memorization, is the learning approach.

Many people are afraid to write because they are afraid to make mistakes. Sentence combining is a way to reduce this fear. Because the content of writing is provided by exercises, a person can focus undivided attention on making clear, correct sentences. Fear is naturally reduced as sentence-making skills and awareness of vocabulary improve.

SC practice brings mistakes out in the open so that a person can *learn* from them. For this reason, mistakes should be welcomed and carefully studied. Each mistake conquered is a threshold that a person crosses—another step toward mature skills and increased self-confidence in writing. SC exercises are simply a way for people to *teach themselves* about "the basics" of words and sentences.

MASTERING VOCABULARY THROUGH SENTENCE COMBINING

Imagine, if you will, a concert guitarist strumming a delicate, familiar melody in a public performance. You're totally relaxed—fully "into" the music—when missed notes begin to interrupt the harmony and rhythm.

What is your automatic reaction? If you're like most people, you'll probably wince inwardly and then start wondering when the *next* mistakes are coming. Because your concentration or mood is broken, you'll then find yourself looking for the nearest exit.

Your reason for reacting this way is hardly difficult to figure out. Generally, whenever you invest time as a listener, you expect a high-quality performance. Since mistakes don't match your expectations, you feel irritated, even cheated, when the musician blows the performance.

Such thoughts parallel the reactions of many readers when they encounter obvious or "dumb" mistakes in writing. Carelessness in writing breaks the reader's concentration or mood. Quite often, the reader's underlying feeling is one of irritation—followed by the "exit response."

Does this mean that mistakes in music—or writing—are always a bad thing? Not at all. When you're *practicing* guitar, writing, or anything else, you're bound to make mistakes. Mistakes provide you with *feedback;* they help you to improve your performance.

The point is that when obvious mistakes occur in a *public* performance, the relationship between you and your audience is weakened, if not destroyed. People who are hearing or reading your work expect you to have worked through your mistakes on your own. It's simply bad form to do your practicing in public.

The purpose of this book is to give you *private* practice with frequently confused words—perhaps the most obvious source of careless writing errors. Some of these words sound alike but have different spellings and meanings.

its	weather
it's	whether
which	miner
witch	minor
coarse	your
course	you're
lessen	who's
lesson	whose

their	to
there	too
they're	two

Other words are quite close in their pronunciation or spelling.

ask	decent
ax(e)	descent
are	accept
our	except
loose	precede
lose	proceed
than	sense
then	since
advice	affect
advise	effect

Such words are tricky. When they're not used with care, they draw attention to themselves, just like missed notes in a musical performance. The "finger exercises" in this book, like practice chords for a guitarist, will help you master such basic vocabulary.

The learning method is a simple, effective one involving four steps:

1. FOCUS on pairs of frequently confused words, concentrating on their definitions.
2. STUDY how the words are used in short sentences, associating the different meanings (and spellings) in context.
3. WRITE one sentence that combines the meanings from the cluster of short sentences, correctly using the words being studied.
4. CHECK your understanding (and spelling) of the words by writing out another, more difficult, sentence.

Let's take a look at how this process works in a few sample exercises.

ILLUSTRATION 1

FOCUS   *Your:* belonging to you
    You're: you are
STUDY   Your language is a tricky one.
    You're going to master its vocabulary.

WRITE   _____ one,

    but _____.

CHECK   Although _____ language is a tricky one,

        _____ going to master its vocabulary.

After focusing on definitions and studying how words such as *your* and *you're* are used in context, the task is to use the *cues,* or hints, provided and write a complete sentence by combining. *This sentence should be written in your own notebook, not in the text.* The next step is mentally to "fill in" the correct words in the CHECK sentence—and then to write out the CHECK sentence in your notebook.
    For the above exercise, your answers should look like this:

WRITE   *Your language is a tricky one,*
    but you're going to master its vocabulary.
CHECK   *Although your language is a tricky one,*
    you're going to master its vocabulary.

Here's a slightly more difficult exercise.

ILLUSTRATION 2

FOCUS   *Sense:* to feel, perceive; something that is reasonable
    Since: connector meaning "because" or expressing time
STUDY   Tony has begun to master vocabulary.
    I sense an improvement in his writing.

WRITE   _____ vocabulary,

    I _____.

CHECK   What I _____, _____ Tony has
    begun to master vocabulary, is an improvement in his
    writing.

In the preceding exercise, the FOCUS word *since* is not included in the STUDY sentences. It's a connecting word, or *connector*, that you must provide in order to do your combining. The logic of the STUDY sentences demands the following writeouts:

WRITE   *Since Tony has begun to master vocabulary,*
　　　　I sense an improvement in his writing.
CHECK   *What I sense, since Tony has begun to master*
　　　　vocabulary, is an improvement in his writing.

Let's now try some combining in which you're working with three frequently confused words. You'll see the word *something* in the first STUDY sentence. Think of this word as a slot into which you'll put information from one or more subsequent sentences.

ILLUSTRATION 3

FOCUS   *Their:* belonging to them
　　　　There: in or at that place; a sentence opener
　　　　They're: they are
STUDY   They're almost sure to hear something.
　　　　Their friends are there in class.

WRITE   _____

　　　　that _____.

CHECK   That _____ friends are _____ in class

　　　　is something _____ almost sure to hear.

In the above illustration, you should use *that* as a connecting word for the *something* slot. Your answers should look like this:

WRITE   *They're almost sure to hear*
　　　　that their friends are there in class.
CHECK   *That their friends are there in class*
　　　　is something they're almost sure to hear.

The word *that* is the most common connector with the *something* slot, but other connectors are also used. In the next illustration, you'll see the word *whether* used as a connector.

ILLUSTRATION 4

FOCUS   *Ask:* to inquire about
       Ax(e): a tool for chopping

       Your: belonging to you
       You're: you are
STUDY   You're going to ask something.
       Do I have your ax(e)?

WRITE   _____

       whether _____.

CHECK   Whether I have _____ _____

       is what _____ going to _____.

Notice, too, that the preceding exercise requires you to change the question—*Do I have your ax(e)?*—into a statement. Here are the answers for that exercise:

WRITE   *You're going to ask*
       whether I have your ax(e).
CHECK   *Whether I have your ax(e)*
       is what you're going to ask.

The use of *something* with a *where* connector is illustrated next. Notice, once again, that a period in the WRITE sentence silently signals you to transform the question—*Where were they wandering?*—into a statement.

ILLUSTRATION 5

FOCUS   *Were:* past tense of *be*
       We're: we are

       Wandering: moving aimlessly
       Wondering: thinking curiously; filled with amazement
STUDY   We're wondering something.
       Where were they wandering together?

WRITE   _____

       _____ together.

CHECK   What _____ _____ is where

they _____ _____ together.

The answers for the above exercise follow; check your writeouts against these:

WRITE   *We're wondering where*
they were wandering together.
CHECK   *What we're wondering is where*
they were wandering together.

So much for exercises with two sentences for combining. Let's now try some three-sentence clusters.

ILLUSTRATION 6

FOCUS   *Are:* present tense of *be*
Our: belonging to us

Coarse: rough, crude
Course: a program; a route; a playing field
STUDY   Words are not allowed on our course.
The words are coarse.
The course is for golf.

WRITE   Words _____

are not _____.

CHECK   On _____ golf _____, _____

words _____ not allowed.

The above exercise requires a *that* or *which* connector. Note: Most instructors prefer a *that* connector because it's the traditional marker for a restrictive (unpunctuated) relative clause. Since no internal punctuation is required in the first writeout, no punctuation clues are provided. Your answers should look like these:

WRITE   *Words that are coarse*
are not allowed on our golf course.
CHECK   *On our golf course, coarse*
words are not allowed.

The next exercise, with more difficult vocabulary, uses the familiar *something* slot; but this one also requires you to supply the correct use of the *except* connector. Try doing it without consulting the answers.

ILLUSTRATION 7

FOCUS   *Confident:* certain; sure of oneself
         Confidant: a close, trusted friend

         Accept: to receive; to approve
         Except: to leave out or take out
STUDY   I'm confident of something.
         My confidant wanted to accept the apology.
         The damage had already been done.

WRITE   I'm _____ apology,

         _____ done.

CHECK   _____ for the fact that the damage had

         already been done, I'm _____ that my

         _____ wanted to _____ the apology.

In the above STUDY sentences, notice that the preposition of needs to be deleted to keep the writeouts grammatical. Notice also that logic requires the *except* connector to be used as follows:

WRITE   *I'm confident that my confidant wanted to accept the apology,*
         except that the damage had already been done.
CHECK   *Except for the fact that the damage had*
         already been done, I'm confident that my
         confidant wanted to accept the apology.

You'll see in the next illustration that the word *something* can also appear at the beginning of a sentence. This often demands what one might call the *it . . . that* pattern of sentence opener:

It's true that . . .

It's entirely likely that . . .

It's regrettably self-evident that . . .

Of course, words other than *that* are often used with *it* at the beginning of a sentence:

It's obvious why . . .

It's still unclear who . . .

It's yet to be decided whether . . .

In the following example, the *it . . . that* pattern is required.

ILLUSTRATION 8

FOCUS *It's:* it is
      Its: belonging to it

      All together: in one place
      Altogether: completely; on the whole
STUDY Something is altogether possible.
      We'll be all together again.
      The prison has its twenty-year reunion.

WRITE _____

     when _____.

CHECK When the prison has _____ twenty-year

    reunion, _____ _____ possible

    that we'll be _____ again.

Compare your writeouts for the above exercise with the answers that follow:

WRITE *It's altogether possible that we'll be all together again*
    when the prison has its twenty-year reunion.
CHECK *When the prison has its twenty-year*
    reunion, it's altogether possible that
    we'll be all together again.

Let's now study an exercise that uses *something* at the beginning of a sentence—but doesn't use some form of *it* construction. Here the word *something* and the verb form are deleted, leaving only a phrase to be combined with the remaining sentences.

ILLUSTRATION 9

FOCUS   *Hour:* sixty minutes
   Our: belonging to us

   Access: the ability to approach or enter
   Excess: more than necessary or usual
STUDY   Something will happen during this hour.
   They are strictly limiting our access.
   The access is to doughnuts.
   The doughnuts are excess ones.

WRITE   During _____, they _____

_____.

CHECK   _____ _____ to _____
   doughnuts will be strictly limited during this

   _____.

Here are the answers for the preceding exercises:

WRITE   *During this hour, they are strictly limiting*
   our access to excess doughnuts.
CHECK   *Our access to excess doughnuts will be*
   strictly limited during this hour.

   A final exercise, with six FOCUS words, follows. After studying the words and their definitions, try to make writeouts on your own, using the clues provided.

ILLUSTRATION 10

FOCUS   *Too:* denoting excess
   Two: a couple

   Inane: stupid
   Insane: crazy

Precede: to come before
Proceed: to go on, continue

STUDY   She'll precede her talk with two jokes.
    The jokes are insane.
    She'll then proceed to answer questions.
    Most will be too inane to ignore.

WRITE   She'll _____

    and _____,

    most of which _____.

CHECK   _____ _____ jokes will

    _____ her talk; then she'll _____

    to answer questions—most _____ _____
    to ignore.

Important punctuation cues are provided in this exercise. Be alert to punctuation in the answers that follow.

WRITE   *She'll precede her talk with two insane jokes*
    and then proceed to answer questions,
    most of which will be too inane to ignore.
CHECK   *Two insane jokes will precede her talk; then*
    she'll proceed to answer questions—most too
    inane to ignore.

Now that you have seen how the exercises work, you're perhaps wondering if that's all there is to "mastering" basic vocabulary.

Not exactly.

Each sequence of ten exercises is followed by a Mastery Quiz. This quiz doesn't ask you to tell what you've learned; it asks you to *show* your understanding of the words you've studied.

The quiz items are set up in the familiar CHECK format. The difference, however, is that quiz items require you to fill in correct words from *memory.* To the extent you're able to do this, you're demonstrating an initial mastery of basic vocabulary.

Sentences in the Mastery Quiz should be written out in your own notebook, not in the text. To check your understanding of words in the ten illustration exercises, try your hand at the following quiz items *without looking back at the original exercises.*

MASTERY QUIZ

1. _____ language is a tricky one; however, _____ going to master its vocabulary. (your, you're)

2. I _____ an improvement in Tony's writing _____ he has begun to master vocabulary. (sense, since)

3. What _____ sure to hear is that _____ friends are _____ in class. (their, there, they're)

4. _____ going to _____ about _____ _____. (ask, ax(e); your, you're)

5. Their _____ together is what _____ _____ about. (were, we're; wandering, wondering)

6. _____ words _____ not allowed on _____ golf _____. (are, our; coarse, course)

7. My _____ wanted to _____ the apology, _____ that the damage had already been done. (confidant, confident; accept, except)

8. Possibly we'll be _____ again when the prison has _____ twenty-year reunion. (its, it's; all together, altogether)

9. They are strictly limiting _____ _____ to _____ doughnuts during this _____. (hour, our; access, excess)

10. Before _____ to answer questions—most of which will be _____ _____ to ignore—she's _____ her talk with _____ _____ jokes. (too, two; inane, insane; preceding, proceeding)

As you can see by examining the Mastery Quiz closely, the items are slightly different forms of WRITE and CHECK sentences that you worked earlier. Your task is to remember the content of previous sentences as well as the FOCUS words you've studied.

Notice also that certain items—5, 7, and 8, for example—have fewer blanks than words to go in them. While these may look easier than the others, they still require you to discriminate between frequently confused words and put the right word in the right spot. Also, notice that item 10 uses a different form of FOCUS words (*preceding, proceeding*) than you studied in the original exercise.

Here are the answers for the Mastery Quiz. Check your sentences against these:

1. *Your* language is a tricky one; however, *you're* going to master its vocabulary.
2. I *sense* an improvement in Tony's writing *since* he has begun to master vocabulary.
3. What *they're* almost sure to hear is that *their* friends are *there* in class.
4. *You're* going to *ask* about *your ax(e)*.
5. Their *wandering* together is what *we're wondering* about.
6. *Coarse* words *are* not allowed on *our* golf *course*.
7. My *confidant* wanted to accept the apology, *except* that the damage had already been done.
8. Possibly we'll be *all together* again when the prison has *its* twenty-year reunion.
9. They are strictly limiting *our access* to *excess* doughnuts during this *hour*.
10. Before *proceeding* to answer questions—most of which will be *too inane* to ignore—she's *preceding* her talk with *two insane* jokes.

FINAL SUGGESTIONS

To help you get the most out of the exercises in this text, here are a few common-sense hints that other students have found useful.

1. Don't rush through the exercises or do them carelessly. The point is to master basic vocabulary and make good sentences *simultaneously*. Concentrate on what you're doing.
2. Whisper the sentences to yourself. *Hearing* sentences and *seeing* patterns will develop your *sentence sense*—an improved feeling for structure, punctuation, and correct use of frequently confused words.

3. Resist the temptation to rely on someone else's work. Take the Mastery Quiz immediately after completing a section of ten exercises; keep track of your progress on the Mastery Quiz Record following this introduction.

4. Be alert to this book's basic vocabulary in your outside reading. Each time you spot one of the frequently confused words you're studying, concentrate on its use in context to reinforce your learning.

5. Use this book's index to identify words you're uncertain about. The index specifies the exercise number(s) that will give you practice with words you've targeted.

6. *Remember to concentrate on basic vocabulary in the real writing that you do on your own.* It's *you,* after all, who has to transfer what you've learned to your written work. That's what *Mastering Basic Vocabulary* is all about.

MASTERY QUIZ RECORD*

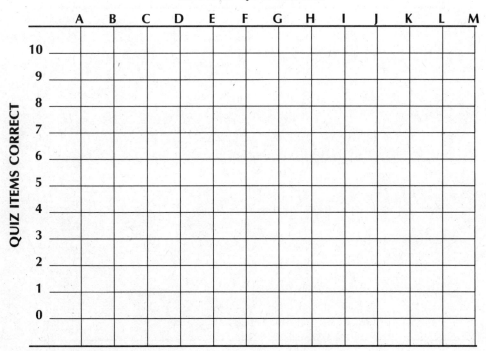

*Note: All parts of the Mastery Quiz sentence must be filled in correctly for an item to be counted as correct.

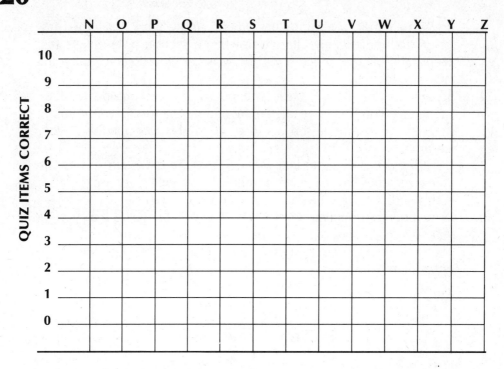

The answer key for all MASTERY QUIZ exercises is available from your instructor.

SEQUENCE A EXERCISES

A•1   your, you're
A•2   loose, lose
A•3   vain, vein
A•4   flour, flower
A•5   lessen, lesson
A•6   its, it's
A•7   pray, prey
A•8   access, excess
A•9   crews, cruise
A•10 affect, effect

A•1

FOCUS   *Your:* belonging to you
    You're: you are

STUDY   Your task is to remember something.
    You're means "you are."

WRITE   _____

    that _____.

CHECK   Remembering that _____

    means "you are" is _____
    task.

A•2

FOCUS   *Loose:* free, escaped; unbound, not tight
    Lose: to mislay, become unable to find

STUDY   The snake got loose yesterday.
    I didn't want to lose it.

WRITE   When _____,

    I _____.

CHECK   I didn't want to _____

    the snake that got _____
    yesterday.

A•3

FOCUS   *Vain:* proud; unsuccessful, futile
    Vein: a blood vessel

STUDY   The student nurse searched in vain.
    He tried to find a blood vein.

WRITE   The _____,

    trying _____.

CHECK   The student nurse's attempt

    to find a blood _____ was

    in _____.

21

A•4

FOCUS *Flour:* ground grain
       Flower: a blossom
STUDY I'll trade you a flower bouquet.
       The trade is for a cup of wheat flour.

WRITE I'll _____

       for _____.

CHECK For a cup of wheat _____,

       I'll trade you a _____ bouquet.

A•5

FOCUS *Lessen:* to diminish
       Lesson: an assignment to be studied
STUDY A lesson would lessen his loneliness.
       The lesson would be on interpersonal communication.

WRITE An interpersonal communication _____

       _____.

CHECK His loneliness would _____

       with a _____ on interpersonal communication.

A•6

FOCUS *Its:* belonging to it
       It's: it is
STUDY It's encouraging to know something.
       Your brain has focused its undivided attention.

WRITE _____

       that _____.
CHECK That your brain has focused

       _____ undivided attention is encouraging to know.

A•7

FOCUS *Pray:* to petition (God); to offer a prayer
Prey: to hunt; to victimize

STUDY Ranchers gathered to pray for something.
Wolves would not prey on their sheep.

WRITE Ranchers _____

that _____.

CHECK Not wanting wolves to

_____ on their sheep, ranch-

ers gathered to _____.

A•8

FOCUS *Access:* the ability to approach or enter
Excess: more than necessary or usual

STUDY I'd like access to your money.
You have money in excess.

WRITE I'd _____,

which _____.

CHECK Your _____ money is

what I'd like _____ to.

A•9

FOCUS *Crews:* sailors
Cruise: a voyage

STUDY The navy's crews are back in port.
They had a cruise in the Caribbean.

WRITE The _____

after _____.

CHECK After a Caribbean _____,

the navy's _____ are back in port.

A•10

FOCUS *Affect:* to influence (used here as a verb)
Effect: result (used here as a noun)

STUDY Smiles affect one's mood positively.
The effect of a frown is just the opposite.

WRITE Smiles _____,

but _____.

CHECK Smiles _____ one's mood positively; however, the

_____ of a frown is just the opposite.

MASTERY QUIZ A

To demonstrate your mastery of words in Sequence A exercises, write out the following sentences in your own notebook, with the correct words filled in. (Do not check back to the exercises for definitions.)

1. Remember _____ task: that _____ means "you are." (your, you're)

2. Yesterday, I didn't want to _____ the snake when it got _____. (loose, lose)

3. Trying to find a blood _____, the student nurse searched in _____. (vain, vein)

4. How about trading a _____ bouquet for a cup of wheat _____? (flour, flower)

5. You can _____ your loneliness with an interpersonal communication _____. (lessen, lesson)

6. _____ encouraging to know that your brain's undivided attention has been focused. (its, it's)

7. So that wolves would not _____ on their sheep, ranchers gathered to _____. (pray, prey)

8. _____ money is something I'd like _____ to. (access, excess)

9. The navy's _____ had a Caribbean _____, but they are now back in port. (crews, cruise)

10. While smiles _____ one's mood positively, the _____ of a frown is just the opposite. (affect, effect)

SEQUENCE B EXERCISES

B•1	wade, weighed
B•2	than, then
B•3	profit, prophet
B•4	knead, need
B•5	discussed, disgust
B•6	dual, duel
B•7	affect, effect
B•8	wear, were, where
B•9	scene, seam, seem
B•10	quiet, quit, quite

B•1

FOCUS   *Wade:* to walk through water, snow, or mud
Weighed: measured as to weight

STUDY   I was first weighed.
I was then ordered to wade ashore.

WRITE   _____,

then _____.

CHECK   After first being _____,

I was then ordered to _____ ashore.

B•2

FOCUS   *Than:* introduces second element in a comparison
Then: at that time

STUDY   The rain then turned to snow.
The rain was heavier than expected.

WRITE   _____, which _____

_____, _____ snow.

CHECK   Heavier _____ expected, the rain _____ turned to snow.

B•3

FOCUS   *Profit:* gains—usually money
Prophet: a foreteller

STUDY   My stock profits soared.
I listened to the prophet's advice.

WRITE   My _____

as _____.

CHECK   The _____'s advice caused my stock _____ to soar.

25

B•4

FOCUS *Knead:* to press or squeeze (dough)
Need: require
STUDY The baker needed money for food.
He kneaded dough faster.

WRITE Because _____,

he _____.

CHECK The baker, who _____

money for food, _____
dough faster.

B•5

FOCUS *Discussed:* talked about, considered
Disgust: loathing, dislike
STUDY She showed disgust for her husband.
The jury discussed this at some length.

WRITE She _____—

a fact that _____.

CHECK The _____ that she showed for her husband was

_____ by the jury at some length.

B•6

FOCUS *Dual:* two
Duel: combat
STUDY The gladiator had dual motives.
He agreed to a "doubleheader" duel.

WRITE _____, who _____

_____, had _____.

CHECK Because he had _____ motives, the gladiator agreed

to a "doubleheader" _____.

B•7

FOCUS *Affect:* to influence (used here as a verb)
Effect: result (used here as a noun)
STUDY We had hoped to affect voter attitudes.
The effect of our ads was disappointing.

WRITE We _____,

but _____.

CHECK While our hope was to

_____ voter attitudes, the

_____ of our ads was disappointing.

B•8

FOCUS *Wear:* to carry on one's body; to weaken, harass
Were: past tense of *be*
Where: in or at what place
STUDY They were asking something.
Where can they wear their outfits?

WRITE They _____

_____ outfits.

CHECK _____ they can _____

their outfits is what they _____ asking.

B•9

FOCUS *Scene:* a view or event
  Seam: the line made by joined edges
  Seem: to appear
STUDY I seem to have created a scene.
  I split my bathing suit's seam.

WRITE I _____

  by _____.

CHECK What I _____ to have

  created by splitting the _____ of my bathing suit is a

  _____.

B•10

FOCUS *Quiet:* silent
  Quit: leave, resign
  Quite: completely, really, truly
STUDY The office is so quiet.
  We'd quite like to quit.

WRITE Because _____,

  we'd _____.

CHECK The office is so _____

  that we'd _____ like to

  _____.

MASTERY QUIZ B

To demonstrate your mastery of words in Sequence B exercises, write out the following sentences in your own notebook, with the correct words filled in. (Do not check back to the exercises for definitions.)

1. I was ordered to _____ ashore after first being _____. (wade, weighed)

2. The rain was heavier _____ expected; _____ it turned to snow. (than, then)

3. Advice from the _____ helped my stock _____ to soar. (profit, prophet)

4. His _____ for money caused the baker to _____ dough faster. (knead, need)

5. Her _____ for her husband was _____ by the jury at some length. (discussed, disgust)

6. Having _____ motives, the gladiator agreed to a "double-header" _____. (dual, duel)

7. To _____ voter attitudes was our aim, but this _____ was not accomplished. (affect, effect)

8. What they _____ asking was: _____ can we _____ our outfits? (wear, were, where)

9. A split _____ in my bathing suit _____ to have created a _____. (scene, seam, seems)

10. We'd _____ like to _____ with the office so _____. (quiet, quit, quite)

SEQUENCE C EXERCISES

C•1	win, wine, whine
C•2	sweet, suit, suite
C•3	were, we're, where
C•4	threw, though, through
C•5	your, you're
C•6	its, it's
C•7	lacks, lax
C•8	loose, lose
C•9	affect, effect
C•10	who's, whose

C•1

FOCUS *Win:* to gain a victory; to obtain
Wine: an alcoholic drink
Whine: a whimper, cry

STUDY Ted began to whine soulfully.
He didn't win the wine.

WRITE Ted _____

because _____.

CHECK It was because Ted didn't

_____ the _____ that

he began to _____ soulfully.

C•2

FOCUS *Sweet:* luscious, fragrant, pleasing
Suit: a set of clothing
Suite: a hotel room

STUDY Your suit was found in our suite.
It was not smelling too sweet.

WRITE _____, which _____

_____, was found _____.

CHECK It was in our _____

that your _____, which

was not smelling too _____, was found.

C•3

FOCUS *Were:* past tense of *be*
We're: we are
Where: in or at what place

STUDY Tomorrow we're going to ask something.
Just where were the valuables stored?

WRITE   Tomorrow _____

_____.

CHECK   Just _____ the valua-

bles _____ stored is what

_____ going to ask to-

morrow.

C·4

FOCUS   *Threw:* hurled
   Though: connector meaning "in
   spite of the fact"
   Through: in one side, out the
   other; finished
STUDY   Somebody threw me the
   frisbee.
   I had said I was all through.

WRITE   Somebody _____

even _____.

CHECK   Even _____ I had said

I was all _____, some-

body _____ me the fris-

bee.

C·5

FOCUS   *Your:* Belonging to you
   You're: you are
STUDY   You're going to master trou-
   blesome words.
   Your practice will be relentless.
   The practice is with basic
   vocabulary.

WRITE   _____

because _____.

CHECK   It's because of _____

relentless   practice   with   basic

vocabulary that _____
going   to   master   troublesome
words.

C·6

FOCUS   *Its:* belonging to it
   It's: it is
STUDY   It's important to remember
   something.
   Its means "belonging to it."
   It's means "it is."

WRITE   _____

that _____,

whereas _____.

CHECK   Remembering that _____
means   "belonging   to   it"   and

that _____ means "it is"
is important.

C·7

FOCUS   *Lacks:* is deficient in, is
   without
   Lax: loose, slack
STUDY   He has self-discipline.
   His self-discipline is lax.
   He lacks moral standards.

WRITE   He not only _____,

but he also _____.

CHECK   He has _____ self-

discipline; hence, he _____
moral standards.

C•8

FOCUS *Loose:* free, escaped; unbound, not tight
Lose: to mislay, become unable to find

STUDY Certain players decided to "get loose."
They "got loose" before the game.
This caused their team to lose.

WRITE Certain _____,

    which _____.

CHECK In deciding to "get _____"
before the game, certain players

    caused their team to _____.

C•9

FOCUS *Affect:* To influence (used here as a verb)
Effect: result (used here as a noun)

STUDY Taxes affect everybody.
The taxes are increased.

The effect on the poor is disastrous.

WRITE Increased _____,

    but _____.

CHECK While increased taxes

    _____ everybody, the

    _____ on the poor is
disastrous.

C•10

FOCUS *Who's:* who is
Whose: belonging to what person

STUDY Marie wants to know something.
Marie is now our leader.
Whose vote was cast against her?

WRITE Marie, _____,

    wants _____.

CHECK Our leader, Marie, wants to

    know _____ vote was cast
against her.

MASTERY QUIZ C

To demonstrate your mastery of words in Sequence C exercises, write out the following sentences in your own notebook, with the correct words filled in. (Do not check back to the exercises for definitions.)

1. Not to _____ the _____ caused Ted to _____ soulfully. (win, wine, whine)

2. We found your _____—not smelling too _____—in our _____. (sweet, suit, suite)

3. _____ asking a question tomorrow: Just _____ _____ the valuables stored? (were, we're, where)

4. I had said I was all _____, but somebody _____ me the frisbee. (threw, though, through)

5. _____ mastering troublesome words with _____ relentless practice. (your, you're)

6. To remember that _____ means "belonging to it" and that _____ means "it is" is important. (its, it's)

7. His _____ self-discipline means that he _____ standards. (lacks, lax)

8. Before the game, certain players "got _____," causing their team to _____. (loose, lose)

9. Increased taxes _____ everybody; however, their _____ on the poor is disastrous. (affect, effect)

10. It's Marie, _____ now our leader, who wants to know _____ vote was cast against her. (who's, whose)

SEQUENCE D EXERCISES

D·1   its, it's
D·2   allot, a lot
D·3   mind, mine
D·4   who's, whose
D·5   their, there, they're
D·6   to, too, two
D·7   well, we'll, will
D·8   decent, descent, dissent
D·9   setting, settling, sitting
D·10   breadth, breath, breathe

D·1

FOCUS   *Its:* belonging to it
    It's: it is
STUDY   It's easy to remember something.
    It's means "it is."
    Its signals possession.

WRITE   _____

    that _____,

    whereas _____.

CHECK   Remembering that _____

    means "it is" and that _____

    signals possession is easy.

D·2

FOCUS   *Allot:* to distribute shares; to set apart
    A lot: a great amount; a plot of ground

STUDY   Let's allot a lot of money.
    The allotment will be for a lot.
    We can build on the lot.

WRITE   Let's _____

    so that _____.

CHECK   To acquire _____ for

    building, we should _____

    _____ of money.

D·3

FOCUS   *Mind:* brain, thoughts
    Mine: belonging to me; a large excavation, pit
STUDY   The mine owner talked with Mina.
    The mine owner is a friend of mine.
    Mina had a mind to strike.

WRITE   The _____, _____,

    talked _____.

33

CHECK Mina had a _____ to strike, but the _____ owner, a friend of _____, talked with her.

CHECK If _____ grades are in jeopardy—or if _____ in a mood to cooperate—_____ is absolute silence _____.

D•4

FOCUS *Who's:* who is
Whose: belonging to what person
STUDY The cooks want to know something.
Who's best among them?
The cooks' recipes all taste the same.

WRITE The cooks, _____,

want _____.

CHECK The question of _____

best is what the cooks, _____ recipes all taste the same, want answered.

D•5

FOCUS *Their:* belonging to them
There: in or at that place; a sentence opener
They're: they are
STUDY There is absolute silence there.
They're in the mood to cooperate.
Their grades are in jeopardy.

WRITE _____

when _____

or when _____.

D•6

FOCUS *To:* a preposition meaning "toward"; an infinitive marker
Too: denoting excess
Two: a couple
STUDY *Two* is a simple word.
It seems all too easy to confuse.
The confusion is with its two sound-alikes.

WRITE _____

that _____

with _____.

CHECK It seems all _____ easy

_____ confuse _____,

a simple word, with its _____ sound-alikes.

D•7

FOCUS *Well:* in a good manner; a hole in the ground
We'll: we will
Will: desire; a legal document; a man's name
STUDY Will said something.
We'll never read the will.
It was thrown down the well.

WRITE _____

because _____.

CHECK "Since the _____ was

thrown down the _____,"

_____ said, "_____
never read it."

into the crevasse doesn't sound

_____, so I _____
on it.

D•8

FOCUS *Decent:* correct, right,
proper
Descent: a drop; a move in a
downward direction
Dissent: to disagree with, protest
STUDY I dissent on the plan.
The plan is for a descent into
the crevasse.
It doesn't sound decent.

WRITE I _____

because _____.

CHECK The plan for a _____

D•9

FOCUS *Setting:* scenery, background
Settling: calming, reassuring
Sitting: resting in an upright po-
sition
STUDY Sitting was a settling ex-
perience.
The sitting was in a setting.
The setting was calm.

WRITE Sitting in _____

was a _____.

CHECK The _____ was calm,

so _____ in it was a

_____ experience.

D•10

FOCUS   *Breadth:* width, scope
        Breath: air taken into the lungs
        and let out
        Breathe: to inhale and exhale
STUDY   It was difficult to breathe.
        His breadth was wide.
        His breath smelled of garlic.

WRITE   It _____

        because _____

        and _____.

CHECK   Because his _____

        was wide and his _____
        smelled of garlic, it was difficult

        to _____.

MASTERY QUIZ D

To demonstrate your mastery of words in Sequence D exercises, write out the following sentences in your own notebook, with the correct words filled in. (Do not check back to the exercises for definitions.)

1. _____ signals possession, and _____ means "it is." (its, it's)

2. If we _____ _____ of money, we'll acquire _____ for building. (allot, a lot)

3. A friend of _____, the _____ owner, talked with Mina, who had a _____ to strike. (mind, mine)

4. The cooks, _____ recipes all taste the same, want an answer to their question: _____ best among us? (who's, whose)

5. It's only when _____ in a mood to cooperate or when _____ grades are in jeopardy that _____ is absolute silence _____. (their, there, they're)

6. _____ confuse _____ with its _____ sound-alikes seems all _____ easy. (to, too, two)

7. According to _____, _____ never be able to read the _____ because it was thrown down the _____. (well, we'll; Will, will)

8. The planned _____ into the crevasse doesn't sound _____; hence, I want to _____. (decent, descent, dissent)

9. A calm _____ made _____ a _____ experience. (setting, settling, sitting)

10. His wide _____ and unpleasant _____ made it difficult to _____. (breadth, breath, breathe)

SEQUENCE E EXERCISES

E•1   their, they're; ask, ax(e)
E•2   your, you're; coarse, course
E•3   he'll, hill; ant, aunt
E•4   maid, made; a rest, arrest
E•5   hear, here; him, hymn
E•6   its, it's; fair, fare
E•7   scene, seen; which, witch
E•8   knew, new; knot, not
E•9   bare, bear; quiet, quite
E•10   girl, grill; one, won

E•1

FOCUS   *Their:* belonging to them
         They're: they are

         Ask: to inquire about
         Ax(e): a tool for chopping
STUDY   They're going to ask something.
         Where is their ax(e) located?

WRITE   _____

         where _____ is located.

CHECK   What _____ going to

         _____ is where _____

         _____ is located.

E•2

FOCUS   *Your:* belonging to you
         You're: you are

Coarse: rough, crude
Course: a program; a route; a playing field
STUDY   You're coarse in your teaching style.
         Your course of study is most interesting.

WRITE   Although _____,

         _____.

CHECK   _____ _____ of study is most interesting—perhaps because _____

         _____ in _____

         teaching style.

E•3

FOCUS   *He'll:* he will
         Hill: mound smaller than a mountain

38

Ant: insect
Aunt: female relative
STUDY   He'll study the ant hill.
The ant hill is his aunt's.

WRITE   _____,

which _____.

CHECK   His _____'s _____

_____ is what _____
be studying.

E•4

FOCUS   *Maid:* unmarried woman; female servant
Made: created; brought about

A rest: some relaxation, a nap
Arrest: to halt, apprehend; the act of apprehending
STUDY   The meter maid took a rest.
Then she made the arrest.

WRITE   After taking _____,

the _____.

CHECK   The _____ was _____

by the meter _____, who

had first taken _____.

E•5

FOCUS   *Hear:* to listen to
Here: in this place

Him: that man
Hymn: a sacred song
STUDY   Let's hear him sing the hymn.
He came here to sing for us.

WRITE   Let's _____

that _____.

CHECK   Because he came _____

to sing for us, let's _____

_____ sing the _____.

E•6

FOCUS   *Its:* belonging to it
It's: it is

Fair: beautiful; just, right
Fare: price charged for transporting a passenger
STUDY   Something is simply not fair.
The bus company is raising its fare.

WRITE   _____

that _____.

CHECK   The fact the bus company is

raising _____ _____

is simply not _____.

E•7

FOCUS   *Scene:* a sight; part of a play
Seen: observed

Which: what one of several
Witch: a practicer of magic; an old, ugly woman
STUDY   They've seen Shakespeare's *Macbeth.*
It opens with a famous witch scene.

WRITE   They've _____,

_____.

CHECK   Shakespeare's   *Macbeth,*

_____ opens with a fa-

mous _____ _____,

is a play they've _____.

E•8

FOCUS   *Knew:* perceived or under-
stood
New: fresh or unused

Knot: a cord or rope tied
Not: a word used to express the
negative
STUDY   I already knew the knot.
It was not new to me.

WRITE   _____;

therefore, _____.

CHECK   Because I already _____

the _____, it was _____

_____ to me.

E•9

FOCUS   *Bare:* naked
Bear: an animal; to carry

Quiet: silent
Quite: truly, completely, entirely
STUDY   The bear was quiet.
I was quite bare.

WRITE   The _____,

and _____.

CHECK   Because I was _____

_____, the _____

was _____.

E•10

FOCUS   *Girl:* a young female
Grill: to broil; question relent-
lessly

One: a single unit; a certain
person
Won: finished first; succeeded;
gained
STUDY   One girl saw who won.
The girl was behind the grill.

WRITE   _____;

she _____.

CHECK   Behind the _____,

_____ _____ saw

who _____.

MASTERY QUIZ E

To demonstrate your mastery of words in Sequence E exercises, write out the following sentences in your own notebook, with the correct words filled in. (Do not check back to the exercises for definitions.)

1. The location of _____ _____ is what _____ going to _____ about. (their, they're; ask, ax(e))

2. _____ _____ style of teaching makes _____ _____ of study most interesting. (your, you're; coarse, course)

3. The _____ _____ that belongs to his _____ is what _____ study. (he'll, hill; ant, aunt)

4. The meter _____ took _____—and then _____ the _____. (maid, made; a rest, arrest)

5. He came _____ to sing for us, so let's _____ _____ sing the _____. (hear, here; him, hymn)

6. For the bus company to raise _____ _____ is simply not _____. (its, it's; fair, fare)

7. A play that they've _____ is Shakespeare's *Macbeth*, _____ opens with a famous _____ _____. (scene, seen; which, witch)

8. The _____ was _____ _____ to me because I already _____ it. (knew, new; knot, not)

9. I was _____ _____; therefore, the _____ was _____. (bare, bear; quiet, quite)

10. A _____—the _____ behind the _____—saw who _____. (girl, grill; one, won)

SEQUENCE F EXERCISES

F•1   hear, here; their, they're
F•2   none, nun; patience, patients
F•3   all ready, already; hair, here
F•4   chef, chief; stake, steak
F•5   presence, presents; your, you're
F•6   allowed, aloud; miner, minor
F•7   read, red; one, won
F•8   plain, plane; wood, would
F•9   formally, formerly; mail, male
F•10   angel, angle; statue, stature

F•1

FOCUS   *Hear:* to listen to
        Here: in this place

        Their: belonging to them
        They're: they are
STUDY   I hear something from their friends.
        They're going to be here at noon.

WRITE   I _____

        that _____.

CHECK   From _____ friends I

      _____ that _____ go-

ing to be _____ at noon.

F•2

FOCUS   *None:* zero, not any
        Nun: a female bound to a religious order

Patience: calmness
Patients: sick persons receiving care
STUDY   Our patients have patience.
        The nun has none.

WRITE   Although _____,

    _____.

CHECK   The _____ has _____

      of the _____ that our

      _____ have.

F•3

FOCUS   *All ready:* prepared
        Already: by or before given time

        Hair: a threadlike growth from skin
        Here: at this place
STUDY   They're already here in the salon.
        They're all ready to trim hair.

WRITE They're _____

and _____.

CHECK _____ _____ in

the salon, they're _____ to

trim _____.

F•4

FOCUS *Chef:* a cook
      Chief: main, primary; a leader

      Stake: a wager; a piece of wood;
      at risk
      Steak: meat
STUDY The chief chef's reputation
      is at stake.
      She serves only hamburger steak.

WRITE The _____

because _____.
CHECK As a result of serving only

hamburger _____, the

reputation of the _____

_____ is at _____.

F•5

FOCUS *Presence:* being present
      Presents: gifts

      Your: belonging to you
      You're: you are
STUDY Your presence at the party
      is expected.
      You're not expected to bring
      presents.

WRITE _____,

but _____.

CHECK While _____ _____

is expected at the party,

_____ not expected to

bring _____.

F•6

FOCUS *Allowed:* permitted
Aloud: not silently

Miner: worker in mines
Minor: one who is underage; a musical term; less important

STUDY The miner was allowed to sing aloud.
He sang in a minor key.

WRITE The _____

in _____.

CHECK The _____, who sang in

a _____ key, was _____

to sing _____.

F•7

FOCUS *Read:* looked at; perused
Red: a color

One: a single unit; a certain person
Won: finished first; succeeded; gained

STUDY One of us blushed red.
We read what we had won.

WRITE _____

when _____.

CHECK As we _____ what we

had _____, _____ of

us blushed _____.

F•8

FOCUS *Plain:* clear, simple
Plane: a tool for woodworking; aircraft; flat, level surface

Wood: a thick collection of trees; lumber, timber
Would: will

STUDY The teacher's point was made very plain.
The plane would be used only on wood.

WRITE The teacher's point—that

_____

_____—

was _____.

CHECK It was made very _____

by the teacher that the _____

_____ be used only on

_____.

F•9

FOCUS *Formally:* correctly; in a dignified way
Formerly: earlier

Mail: letters, packages; flexible armor
Male: of the masculine sex; a man

STUDY Carol was formally introduced to a male.
The male had formerly been a mail man.

WRITE Carol _____

who _____.

CHECK A _____, who had

_____ been a _____

man, was _____ introduced to Carol.

F•10

FOCUS   *Angel:* a messenger of God
      Angle: a slant

      Statue: a solid carving or model
      Stature: standing, quality
STUDY   The angel's statue stands at
      an angle.

      It adds stature to the entryway.

WRITE   Standing _____,

      the _____

      and _____.

CHECK   The _____'s _____

      stands at an _____, add-

      ing _____ to the entryway.

MASTERY QUIZ F

To demonstrate your mastery of words in sequence F exercises, write out the following sentences in your own notebook, with the correct words filled in. (Do not check back to the exercises for definitions.)

1. _____ going to be _____ at noon, according to _____ friends. (hear, here; their, they're)

2. Our _____ have _____, but the _____ has _____. (none, nun; patience, patients)

3. Not only are they _____ _____ in the salon, but they're _____ to trim _____. (all ready, already; hair, here)

4. The _____ _____ serves only hamburger _____; hence, her reputation is at _____. (chef, chief; stake, steak)

5. At the party _____ _____ is expected; however, _____ not expected to bring _____. (presence, presents; your, you're)

6. Singing _____ in a _____ key was what the _____ was _____ to do. (allowed, aloud; miner, minor)

7. Blushing _____, _____ of us _____ what we had _____. (read, red; one, won)

8. The teacher's point was very _____: The _____ _____ _____ be used only on _____. (plain, plane; wood, would)

9. The _____ had _____ been a _____ man; he was _____ introduced to Carol. (formally, formerly; mail, male)

10. Adding _____ to the entryway, the _____'s _____ stands at an _____. (angel, angle; statue, stature)

SEQUENCE G EXERCISES

G·1	scene, seen; quiet, quite
G·2	wander, wonder; gym, Jim
G·3	cause, caws; grisly, grizzly
G·4	scent, sent; teas, tease
G·5	groan, grown; grocer, grosser
G·6	its, it's; plain, plane
G·7	precede, proceed; pretest, protest
G·8	advice, advise; accept, except
G·9	their, there, they're; allowed, aloud
G·10	pleas, please; their, there, they're

G·1

FOCUS   *Scene:* a sight; part of a play
      Seen: observed

      Quiet: silent
      Quite: truly, completely, entirely
STUDY   We had seen a scene.
      The scene was quite quiet.

WRITE   We _____

      that _____.

CHECK   A _____ _____

      _____ was what we had

      _____.

G·2

FOCUS   *Wander:* to move aimlessly
      Wonder: to think curiously; to
      be filled with amazement

Gym: recreation room
Jim: a man's name
STUDY   Jim was wandering around
      the gym.
      He was wondering when prac-
      tice would begin.

WRITE   Jim _____

      and _____.

CHECK   _____ around the

      _____, _____ was

      _____ when practice
      would begin.

G·3

FOCUS   *Cause:* reason
      Caws: cries of crows

      Grisly: frightful
      Grizzly: a bear; gray

47

STUDY   A crow's caws are a little grisly.
A grizzly's claws are cause for alarm.

WRITE   While _____,

a _____.

CHECK   Unlike a crow's _____,

which are only a little _____,

a _____'s claws are _____

for alarm.

G·4

FOCUS   *Scent:* a fragrance
Sent: dispatched

Teas: plural of *tea*—a beverage
Tease: to torment, to irritate

STUDY   Merchants were sent here to tease us.
Their tease was a scent from exotic teas.

WRITE   Merchants _____

with _____.

CHECK   It was with a _____

from exotic _____ that

merchants were _____

here to _____ us.

G·5

FOCUS   *Groan:* deep sigh
Grown: arrived at full maturity

Grocer: merchant
Grosser: coarser, fatter

STUDY   The grocer gave out a groan.
He had grown steadily grosser.

WRITE   _____, who _____

_____, gave _____.

CHECK   Having _____ steadily _____, the _____

gave out a _____.

G·6

FOCUS   *Its:* belonging to it
It's: it is

Plain: clear, simple
Plane: a tool for woodworking; an aircraft; flat, level surface

STUDY   Something is plain to most observers.
The plane's crash resulted from its overload.

WRITE   _____

that _____

CHECK   To most observers, _____

_____ that the _____'s

crash resulted from _____

overload.

G·7

FOCUS   *Precede:* to come before
Proceed: to go on, continue

Pretest: to test in advance (used here as a noun)
Protest: to speak against

STUDY He preceded me on the pretest.
I proceeded to protest.

WRITE He _____;

therefore, I _____.

CHECK Because he _____ me

on the _____, I _____

to _____.

G•8

FOCUS *Advice:* counsel (noun)
Advise: to give advice to (verb)

Accept: to receive, to approve
Except: to leave out or take out
STUDY I'd advise you to accept my recommendations.
This is except when my advice is wrong.

WRITE I'd _____—

_____.

CHECK _____ when my _____

is wrong, I'd _____ you

to _____ my recommendations.

G•9

FOCUS *Their:* belonging to them
There: in or at that place
They're: they are

Allowed: permitted
Aloud: not silently
STUDY Their names are there on the chalkboard.
They're not allowed to talk aloud.

WRITE _____;

hence, _____.

CHECK Because _____ names

are _____ on the chalk-

board, _____ not _____

to talk _____.

G•10

FOCUS *Pleas:* arguments
Please: to delight; a polite addition to requests

Their: belonging to them
They're: they are
STUDY They're out to please their teacher.
Their pleas will go unnoticed.

WRITE _____;

however, _____.

CHECK Although _____ out

to _____ _____

teacher, _____ _____

will go unnoticed.

MASTERY QUIZ G

To demonstrate your mastery of words in Sequence G exercises, write out the following sentences in your own notebook, with the correct words filled in. (Do not check back to the exercises for definitions.)

1. A _____ that was _____ _____ was what we had _____. (scene, seen; quiet, quite)

2. _____ when practice would begin, _____ was _____ around the _____. (wandering, wondering; gym, Jim)

3. A _____'s claws are _____ for alarm, but a crow's _____ are only a little _____. (cause, caws; grisly, grizzly)

4. The _____ from exotic _____ is a _____; that's why merchants were _____ here. (scent, sent; teas, tease)

5. It was the _____, who had _____ steadily _____, that gave out the _____. (groan, grown; grocer, grosser)

6. What is _____ to most observers is that the _____'s crash resulted from _____ overload. (its, it's; plain, plane)

7. I _____ to _____ because he _____ me on the _____. (preceded, proceeded; pretest, protest)

8. _____ my recommendations—that's my _____—_____ when I _____ you wrongly. (advice, advise; accept, except)

9. _____ names are _____ on the chalkboard—which means that _____ not _____ to talk _____. (their, there, they're; allowed, aloud)

10. _____ out to _____ _____ teacher, but _____ will go unnoticed. (pleas, please; their, they're)

SEQUENCE H EXERCISES

H•1	were, we're, where; wandering, wondering
H•2	their, there, they're; weather, whether
H•3	knows, nose; knew, new
H•4	your, you're; roomers, rumors
H•5	certain, curtain; its, it's
H•6	blew, blue; sea, see
H•7	ask, ax(e); read, red
H•8	bald, bawled; baron, barren
H•9	access, excess; when, win
H•10	hear, here; peal, peel

H•1

FOCUS *Were:* past tense of *be*
We're: we are
Where: in or at what place

Wandering: moving aimlessly
Wondering: thinking curiously; filled with amazement

STUDY We're wondering about something.
Just where were they wandering yesterday?

WRITE _____

_____ yesterday.

CHECK What _____ _____

about is just _____ they

_____ _____ yes-
terday.

H•2

FOCUS *Their:* belonging to them
There: in that place, a sentence opener
They're: they are

Weather: condition of the atmosphere
Whether: if

STUDY The weather is so oppressive there.
They're discussing whether to cancel their trip.

WRITE The _____

that _____.

CHECK _____ discussing

_____ to cancel _____

trip because the _____

is so oppressive _____.

51

H·3

FOCUS *Knows:* understands
   Nose: the organ used for smelling

   Knew: perceived or understood
   New: fresh or unused
STUDY Newton knows something for sure.
   We knew about his nose.
   His nose was new.

WRITE Newton _____

   that _____.

CHECK What Newton _____

   for sure is that we _____

   about his _____ _____.

H·4

FOCUS *Your:* belonging to you
   You're: you are

   Roomers: people who rent rooms
   Rumors: talk not based on fact
STUDY From recent rumors I hear something.
   Your roomers are leaving.
   You're raising the rent.

WRITE From _____, _____

   that _____

   because _____.

CHECK Recent _____ suggest

   that _____ _____

   are leaving because _____
   raising the rent.

H·5

FOCUS *Certain:* sure, assured
   Curtain: fabric covering a window or concealing a stage

   Its: belonging to it
   It's: it is
STUDY It's almost certain.
   The theater will close its curtain.
   It's about to go bankrupt.

WRITE _____

   that _____

   because _____.

CHECK Because of _____ near

   bankruptcy, _____ almost

   _____ that the theater will

   close _____ _____.

H·6

FOCUS *Blew:* Past tense of *blow*
   Blue: a color

   Sea: ocean
   See: look at
STUDY The wind blew across the sea.
   The sea was stunningly blue.
   We could see kites going up.

WRITE As _____,

   we _____.

CHECK In the wind that _____

   across the stunningly _____

   _____, we could _____
   kites going up.

H•7

FOCUS *Ask:* to inquire about
       Ax(e): a tool for chopping

       Read: looked at; perused
       Red: a color
STUDY Let's ask about the ax(e).
      The ax(e) is red.
      We've read about it.

WRITE Let's _____

     that _____.

CHECK We've _____ about

     the _____ _____, so

     let's _____ about it.

H•8

FOCUS *Bald:* lacking hair
       Bawled: wept loudly

       Baron: lowest rank of nobility
       Barren: unproductive
STUDY The baron finally bawled
      with emotion.
      The baron was bald.
      His life now seemed barren.

WRITE _____, whose _____

     _____, finally _____.
CHECK Because his life now

     seemed _____, the _____

     _____ finally _____
     with emotion.

H•9

FOCUS *Access:* ability to enter,
      approach

       Excess: more than necessary or
       usual

       When: at what time
       Win: to gain a victory
STUDY Julie wants to know
      something.
      When will she win access?
      The access is to the excess
      peanuts.

WRITE Julie _____

     _____

     _____ peanuts.
CHECK What Julie wants to know is

     _____ she will _____

     _____ to the _____
     peanuts.

H•10

FOCUS *Hear:* to listen to
       Here: in this place

       Peal: a loud ringing sound
       Peel: to pare, cut off the skin
STUDY I stood here on the street.
      I was peeling an orange.
      I could hear bells pealing.

WRITE Standing _____

     and _____,

     I _____.

CHECK _____ on the street,

     as I stood _____ an or-

     ange, I could _____ bells

     _____.

MASTERY QUIZ H

To demonstrate your mastery of words in Sequence H exercises, write out the following sentences in your own notebook, with the correct words filled in. (Do not check back to the exercises for definitions.)

1. Just _____ they _____ _____ yesterday is what _____ _____ about. (were, we're, where; wandering, wondering)

2. With the _____ so oppressive _____, _____ discussing _____ to cancel _____ trip. (their, there, they're; weather, whether)

3. We _____ about Newton's _____ _____—this he _____ for sure. (knows, nose; knew, new)

4. According to recent _____, _____ _____ are leaving because _____ raising the rent. (your, you're; roomers, rumors)

5. The theater is about to go bankrupt; therefore, _____ almost _____ that _____ _____ will close. (certain, curtain; its, it's)

6. The wind _____ across a _____ that was stunningly _____, and we could _____ kites going up. (blew, blue; sea, see)

7. We've _____ about the _____ _____, so let's _____ about it. (ask, ax(e); read, red)

8. The _____ _____ finally _____ with emotion because his life now seemed _____. (bald, bawled; baron, barren)

9. _____ she will _____ _____ to the _____ peanuts is what Julie wants to know. (access, excess; when, win)

10. As I stood _____ on the street _____ an orange, I could _____ bells _____. (hear, here; pealing, peeling)

SEQUENCE I EXERCISES

I•1   all, awl; your, you're
I•2   wear, where; were, we're
I•3   chews, choose; crews, cruise
I•4   hour, our; presence, presents
I•5   forth, fourth; its, it's
I•6   tacks, tax; cents, sense
I•7   him, hymn; chance, chants
I•8   road, rode; rote, wrote
I•9   made, maid; whine, wine
I•10 sail, sale; taught, taut

I•1

FOCUS *All:* everyone
Awl: a sharply pointed tool

Your: belonging to you
You're: you are
STUDY Your awl is a tool.
The tool is dangerous.
You're all going to respect it.

WRITE Since _____,

_____.

CHECK _____ _____

going to respect _____

_____ because it's a dangerous tool.

I•2

FOCUS *Wear:* to carry on one's body; to weaken, harass

Where: in or at what place

Were: past tense of *be*
We're: we are
STUDY We were invited to the play.
We're not sure what to wear.
We're not sure where to go.

WRITE We _____,

but _____

or _____.
CHECK In spite of the fact that we

_____ invited to the play,

_____ not sure what to

_____ or _____

to go.

I•3

FOCUS *Chews:* bites and crushes with the teeth
Choose: to select or decide

55

Crews: sailors
Cruise: voyage

STUDY The captain slowly chews her food.

She wonders which crews to choose.

The crews will be for the next cruise.

WRITE _____, wondering

_____,

slowly _____.

CHECK As she slowly _____ her food, the captain wonders

which _____ to _____

for the next _____.

1·4

FOCUS *Hour:* sixty minutes
Our: belonging to us

Presence: being present
Presents: gifts

STUDY The hour was up.

Our presence was ignored.

Presents were distributed.

WRITE When _____,

_____,

and _____.

CHECK In spite of _____

_____, when the _____

was up, _____ were distributed.

1·5

FOCUS *Forth:* forward, onward
Fourth: following the third

Its: belonging to it
It's: it is

STUDY It's the fourth time.
Our team has gone forth.
It has met its match.

WRITE _____

that _____

and _____.

CHECK For the _____ time,

our team has gone _____

and met _____ match.

I•6

FOCUS *Tacks:* small nails
Tax: a mandatory fee

Cents: coins
Sense: to feel or to perceive;
something that is reasonable

STUDY A tax makes little sense.
The tax is ten cents.
The tax is on thumb tacks.

WRITE A _____

makes _____.

CHECK It makes little _____ to

have a _____ of ten

_____ on thumb _____.

I•7

FOCUS *Him:* that man
Hymn: a sacred song

Chance: accidentally, without
plan
Chants: melodies, songs

STUDY I hired him by chance.
He was hired to sing hymns.
He was hired to sing chants.

WRITE By _____

_____.

CHECK It was by _____ that I

hired _____ to sing _____

and _____.

I•8

FOCUS *Road:* a way made for
traveling
Rode: traveled along; past tense
of *ride*

Rote: a fixed course or proce-
dure; by memory
Wrote: past tense of *write*

STUDY We rode down the road.
He wrote about learning.
The learning was by rote.

WRITE As _____,

he _____.

CHECK What he _____ about,

as we _____ down the

_____, was learning by

_____.

I•9

FOCUS *Made:* created, brought a-
bout
Maid: unmarried woman; female servant

Whine: to whimper, cry
Wine: an alcoholic drink

STUDY   The maid finished off the wine.
The wine was French-made.
She then began to whine for some more.

WRITE   Finishing _____,

the _____.

CHECK The French- _____

_____ was finished

off by the _____, who

then began to _____ for some more.

I•10

FOCUS   *Sail:* the canvas of a boat or ship; to travel in a boat or ship
Sale: to be sold

Taught: instructed
Taut: tight

STUDY   The boat was up for sale.
The crew pulled the sail taut.
The crew was well taught.

WRITE   Although _____,

the crew, _____,

pulled _____.

CHECK   The boat was up for

_____; nevertheless, the

well- _____ crew pulled

the _____ _____.

MASTERY QUIZ I

To demonstrate your mastery of words in Sequence I exercises, write out the following sentences in your own notebook, with the correct words filled in. (Do not check back to the exercises for definitions.)

1. Respect _____ _____—a dangerous tool—is what _____ _____ going to do. (all, awl; your, you're)

2. Although we _____ invited to the play, _____ not sure _____ to go or what to _____. (wear, where; were, we're)

3. Wondering which _____ to _____ for her next _____, the captain slowly _____ her food. (chews, choose; crews, cruise)

4. After the _____ was up, _____ were distributed and _____ _____ was ignored. (hour, our; presence, presents)

5. Our team has gone _____ for the _____ time—and has met _____ match. (forth, fourth; its, it's)

6. The _____ on thumb _____ is ten _____—which makes little _____. (tacks, tax; cents, sense)

7. Hiring _____ to sing _____ and _____ was only by _____. (him, hymns, chance, chants)

8. _____ learning was what he _____ about as we _____ down the _____. (road, rode; rote, wrote)

9. The _____ finished off the French-_____ _____ and then began to _____ for some more. (made, maid; whine, wine)

10. The well-_____ crew pulled the _____ _____—in spite of the fact that the boat was up for _____. (sail, sale; taught, taut)

SEQUENCE J EXERCISES

J•1   its, it's; their, they're
J•2   do, due; sea, see
J•3   sense, since; precede, proceed
J•4   accept, except; one, won
J•5   hear, here; guessed, guest
J•6   were, where; sight, site
J•7   premise, promise; your, you're
J•8   assistance, assistants; knew, new
J•9   who's, whose; pain, pane
J•10 board, bored; hole, whole

J•1

FOCUS   *Its:* belonging to it
    It's: it is

    Their: belonging to them
    They're: they are

STUDY   Something is rather unlikely.
They're coming for their things.
The rain is now at its worst.

WRITE _____

    that _____

    because _____.

CHECK   With the rain now at

    _____ worst, _____

    rather unlikely that _____

    coming for _____ things.

J•2

FOCUS   *Do:* to perform
    Due: owed

    Sea: ocean
    See: look at

STUDY   They do not see something.
The rent on the cottage is al-
ready due.
The cottage is by the sea.

WRITE   They _____

    why _____.

CHECK   Why the rent on the cottage

    by the _____ is already

    _____ is what they _____

    not _____.

J•3

FOCUS *Sense:* to feel, perceive; something that is reasonable
Since: connector meaning "because" or expressing time

Precede: to come before
Proceed: to go on, continue

STUDY I sense something.
Age must precede beauty.
You should proceed first.

WRITE I _____,

you _____.

CHECK It's my _____ that,

_____ age must _____

beauty, you should _____
first.

J•4

FOCUS *Accept:* to receive, to approve
Except: to leave out or take out

One: a single unit; a certain person
Won: finished first; succeeded; gained

STUDY We were ready to accept the contract.
This was except for one item.
The item specified terms if we won.

WRITE We _____

that _____.

CHECK _____ for _____
item that specified terms if we

_____, we were ready to

_____ the contract.

J•5

FOCUS *Hear:* to listen to
Here: in this place

Guessed: speculated about
Guest: a visitor

STUDY I hear something through the grapevine.
The guest has guessed my identity.
The guest was here yesterday.

WRITE I _____

that _____

has _____.

CHECK From what I _____
through the grapevine, the

_____ who was _____

yesterday has _____ my
identity.

J•6

FOCUS *Were:* past tense of *be*
Where: in or at what place

Sight: something seen or worth seeing
Site: location or scene

STUDY We were at a site.
Many had died there.
The sight of it was agonizing.

WRITE We _____;

the _____.

CHECK The _____ of the

_____ _____ many had
died was agonizing to us who

_____ there.

J•7

FOCUS *Premise:* basis for argument
Promise: an agreement to do or not to do something

Your: belonging to you
You're: you are

STUDY Something is your premise.
A promise is a legal contract.
You're likely to be disappointed.

WRITE It's _____

_____,

but _____.

CHECK Although it's _____

_____ that a _____

is a legal contract, _____
likely to be disappointed.

J•8

FOCUS *Assistance:* help, aid
Assistants: helpers, aides

Knew: perceived or understood
New: fresh or unused

STUDY The assistants already knew something.
The assistants were new.
No assistance could be given.

WRITE The _____

that _____.

CHECK No _____ could be

given was what the _____

_____ already _____.

J•9

FOCUS *Who's:* who is
Whose: belonging to what person

Pain: suffering, agony
Pane: a square of glass

STUDY Gerald asked something.
His pain was considerable.
"Who's sweeping up the broken pane?"

WRITE Gerald, _____,

asked, "_____?"

CHECK "_____ sweeping up

the broken _____?" asked

Gerald, _____ _____
was considerable.

J•10

FOCUS *Board:* timber, piece of wood, group of people
Bored: wearied by dullness; pierced

Hole: a hollow place, cavity
Whole: all, entire

STUDY A hole has been bored.
The whole board was ruined.
The board was mahogany.

WRITE Because _____,

the _____.

CHECK A _____ _____

ruined the _____ mahog-

any _____.

MASTERY QUIZ J

To demonstrate your mastery of words in Sequence J exercises, write out the following sentences in your own notebook, with the correct words filled in. (Do not check back to the exercises for definitions.)

1. The rain is now at _____ worst; therefore, _____ unlikely that _____ coming for _____ things. (its, it's; their, they're)

2. Rent on the cottage by the _____ is already _____, but they _____ not _____ why. (do, due; sea, see)

3. You should _____ first—_____ age must _____ beauty. (sense, since; precede, proceed)

4. _____ item in the contract specified terms if we _____; _____ for that, we were willing to _____ it. (accept, except; one, won)

5. Through the grapevine I _____ that my identity has been _____ by the _____ who was _____ yesterday. (hear, here; guessed, guest)

6. The _____ _____ many had died was an agonizing _____ to those of us who _____ there. (were, where; sight, site)

7. _____ likely to be disappointed if _____ _____ is that a _____ is a legal contract. (premise, promise; your, you're)

8. The _____, who were _____, already _____ that no _____ could be given. (assistance, assistants; knew, new)

9. In considerable _____, Gerald asked, "_____ sweeping up the broken _____?" (who's, whose; pain, pane)

10. A _____ had been _____, which ruined the _____ mahogany _____. (board, bored; hole, whole)

SEQUENCE K EXERCISES

K•1   loose, lose; your, you're
K•2   cellar, seller; ware, wear
K•3   your, you're; patience, patients
K•4   loan, lone; kneads, needs
K•5   mind, mine; peace, piece
K•6   profit, prophet; super, supper
K•7   none, nun; pries, prize
K•8   plain, plane; pleas, please
K•9   sense, since; way, weigh
K•10   vain, vane; weather, whether

K•1

FOCUS   *Loose:* free, escaped; unbound, not tight
Lose: to mislay, become unable to find

Your: belonging to you
You're: you are

STUDY   You'll lose your dog.
You're not careful.
You let him get loose.

WRITE   You'll _____

and _____ .

CHECK   If _____ not careful

and let _____ dog get

_____ , you'll _____

him.

K•2

FOCUS   *Cellar:* a room under a house
Seller: one who sells

Ware(s): merchandise
Wear: to carry on one's body; to weaken, harass

STUDY   The seller displayed her wares.
The wares were ready-to-wear.
The display was in a cellar.

WRITE   The _____

_____ .

CHECK   Ready-to _____ _____

were displayed by the _____

in a _____ .

K•3

FOCUS   *Your:* belonging to you
You're: you are

Patience: calmness
Patients: sick persons receiving care

STUDY   I suppose you're canceling our tennis match.
This is just to see your patients.
The patients are running out of patience.

WRITE   I _____

_____,

who _____.

CHECK   I suppose it's just to see

_____ _____, who are

running out of _____, that

_____ canceling our tennis match.

K•4

FOCUS   *Loan:* borrowed money
Lone: single; solitary

Knead: to press or squeeze (dough)
Need: to require

STUDY   A lone baker kneads dough.
He thinks about a loan.
He desperately needs it.

WRITE   As _____,

he _____

that _____.

CHECK   Thinking about a _____

that he desperately _____,

a _____ baker _____
dough.

K•5

FOCUS   *Mind:* brain, thoughts
Mine: belonging to me; a large excavation quarry, pit

Peace: quiet
Piece: a part of something

STUDY   I don't care about maintaining peace.
I gave him a piece of my mind.
I made his things mine.

WRITE   Since _____,

I _____

and _____.

CHECK   Maintaining _____ is not something I care about; therefore, I not only made his

things _____ but also gave

him a _____ of my

_____.

K•6

FOCUS   *Profit:* gains—usually in money
Prophet: a foreteller

Super: amazing, astonishing, great
Supper: an evening meal

STUDY   Profits were not super.

The profits were from the prophet's speech.
They nevertheless bought us supper.

WRITE _____,

but _____.

CHECK   While there were no _____

_____ from the _____

speech, they nevertheless bought

us _____.

K•7

FOCUS   *None:* zero, not any
Nun: a female bound to a religious order

Pries: moves by leverage
Prize: a reward
STUDY   The nun pries open a door.
She is looking for a prize.
She sees none.

WRITE   The _____,

looking _____;

but _____.

CHECK   As she _____ open a

door, the _____ looks for

a _____—but she sees

_____.

K•8

FOCUS   *Plain:* clear, simple
Plane: a tool for woodworking; aircraft; flat, level surface

Pleas: arguments
Please: to delight
STUDY   Please use plain English.
Explain your pleas.
Your pleas are to drop plane geometry.

WRITE _____

to _____

to drop _____.

CHECK   Using _____ English,

_____ explain your _____

to drop _____ geometry.

K•9

FOCUS   *Sense:* to feel, perceive; something that is reasonable
Since: connector meaning "because" or expressing time

Way: a manner of doing things
Weigh: to measure the heaviness of
STUDY   I sense something.
You weigh more than I do.
Your way will probably win out.

WRITE _____ I _____,

your _____ out.

CHECK _____ you _____

more than I do, I _____

that your _____ will probably win out.

K•10

FOCUS   *Vain:* proud; unsuccessful; futile

Vane: a device that shows wind direction

Weather: condition of the atmosphere
Whether: if

STUDY   The newscaster watched the weather vane.
She hoped in vain for overdue rain.
She wondered whether to give up reporting.

WRITE   The _____—
hoping _____
and _____.

CHECK   Watching the _____
_____ and hoping in _____
for overdue rain, the newscaster
wondered _____ to give up
reporting.

MASTERY QUIZ K

To demonstrate your mastery of words in Sequence K exercises, write out the following sentences in your own notebook, with the correct words filled in. (Do not check back to the exercises for definitions).

1. Let _____ dog get _____, and you'll _____ him if _____ not careful. (loose, lose; your, you're)

2. It was in a _____ that the _____ displayed her _____, which were ready-to-_____. (cellar, seller; wares, wear)

3. _____ _____ are running out of _____ so I suppose _____ canceling our tennis match. (your, you're; patience, patients)

4. A _____ baker _____ dough and thinks about a _____ that he desperately _____. (loan, lone; kneads, needs)

5. I don't care about maintaining _____, so I gave him a _____ of my _____ and made his things _____. (mind, mine; peace, piece)

6. _____ from the _____ speech were not _____; nevertheless, they bought us _____. (profits, prophet's; super, supper)

7. After she _____ open a door, the _____ looks for a _____—but she sees _____. (none, nun; pries, prize)

8. _____ explain your _____ to drop _____ geometry in _____ English. (plain, plane; pleas, please)

9. I _____ that your _____ will probably win out _____ you _____ more than I do. (sense, since; way, weigh)

10. The newscaster watched the _____ _____, hoped in _____ for overdue rain, and wondered _____ to give up reporting. (vain, vane; weather, whether)

SEQUENCE L EXERCISES

L·1 aisle, I'll; stairs, stares
L·2 one, won; your, you're
L·3 chased, chaste; knight, night
L·4 faint, feint; scene, seen
L·5 choose, chose; hear, here
L·6 wear, where; were, we're
L·7 guess, guest; hairy, Harry
L·8 ceiling, sealing; staid, stayed
L·9 boarder, border; coarse, course
L·10 its, it's; sense, since

L·1

FOCUS *Aisle:* a narrow passageway
I'll: I will

Stairs: a flight of steps
Stares: gazes (used here as a noun)

STUDY I'll probably get some stares.
I'll race up the stairs.
I'll cartwheel down the aisle.

WRITE I'll _____

when I _____

and _____ .

CHECK After racing up the _____
and cartwheeling down the

_____, _____ prob-

ably get some _____ .

L·2

FOCUS *One:* a single unit; a certain person
Won: finished first; succeeded; gained

Your: belonging to you
You're: you are

STUDY We won your trophy.
There was one reason.
You're a rotten team.

WRITE We _____ :

_____ .

CHECK The _____ reason that

we _____ _____ tro-

phy is that _____ a rotten
team.

69

L•3

FOCUS *Chased:* followed, pursued
Chaste: pure

Knight: title of honor
Night: darkness

STUDY A moon filled the night sky.
The maiden chased the knight.
The maiden was chaste.

WRITE A _____

as _____.

CHECK A _____ maiden _____

the _____ under a moon-

filled _____ sky.

L•4

FOCUS *Faint:* collapse, fall down
in a stupor
Feint: a pretended attack to take
someone off guard

Scene: a sight; part of a play
Seen: observed

STUDY We've seen the scene.
Pam feints for her gun.
Sam faints out of fear.

WRITE We've _____

in which _____

and _____.

CHECK The _____ in which

Pam _____ for her gun

and Sam _____ out of fear

is one that we've _____.

L•5

FOCUS *Choose:* select or decide
Chose: past tense of *choose*

Hear: listen
Here: in this place

STUDY From rumors we hear
something.
Most people chose to live
elsewhere.
Some may still choose to live
here.

WRITE From _____

_____,

although _____.

CHECK Most people _____ to
live elsewhere from rumors that

we _____; some, how-

ever, may still _____ to

live _____.

L•6

FOCUS *Wear:* to carry on one's
body; to weaken, harass
Where: in or at what place

Were: past tense of *be*
We're: we are

STUDY We're asking two questions.
Where were you last night?
What will you wear tonight?

WRITE _____:

_____,

and _____?

CHECK   Two questions—_____

you _____ last night and

what you will _____

tonight—are what _____
asking.

L•7

FOCUS   *Guess:* a speculation
Guest: a visitor

Hairy: covered with hair
Harry: a man's name
STUDY   I'd take a guess on some-
thing.
The guest's name is Harry.
The guest is hairy.

WRITE   I'd _____

that _____.

CHECK   According to my _____,

the name of the _____

_____ is _____.

L•8

FOCUS   *Ceiling:* the overhead surface of a room; the top limit
Sealing: fastening, closing

Staid: sober, solemn, quiet
Stayed: remained
STUDY   The workmen stayed on
ladders.
They were totally staid.
They used sealing material on
the ceiling.

WRITE   The _____

and _____.

CHECK   Using _____ material on the _____, the totally _____ workmen _____ on ladders.

L•9

FOCUS   *Boarder:* a lodger
Border: the outer edge

Coarse: rough, crude
Course: a program; a route; a playing field

STUDY   The boarder followed a course.
The boarder was coarse-mannered.
The course ran along the border.

WRITE   The _____ that _____.

CHECK   Along the _____ ran a _____ that the _____ - mannered _____ followed.

L•10

FOCUS   *Its:* belonging to it
It's: it is

Sense: to feel or perceive; something that is reasonable
Since: connector meaning "because" or expressing time

STUDY   The essay states its point clearly.
The essay makes very good sense.
It's unlikely that it will fail.

WRITE   _____ and _____, _____.

CHECK   _____ unlikely that the essay will fail, _____ it states _____ point clearly and makes very good _____.

MASTERY QUIZ L

To demonstrate your mastery of words in Sequence L exercises, write out the following sentences in your own notebook, with the correct words filled in. (Do not check back to the exercises for definitions.)

1. To get some _____, _____ race up the _____ and cartwheel down the _____. (aisle, I'll; stairs, stares)

2. _____ a rotten team; that's the _____ reason we _____ _____ trophy. (one, won; your, you're)

3. The _____ was _____ by the _____ maiden under a moon-filled _____ sky. (chased, chaste; knight, night)

4. Pam _____ for her gun and Sam _____ out of fear in the _____ that we've _____. (faints, feints; scene, seen)

5. According to rumors we _____, most people _____ to live elsewhere, but some may still _____ to live _____. (choose, chose; hear, here)

6. _____ asking you _____ you _____ last night and what you will _____ tonight. (wear, where; were, we're)

7. The name of the _____ _____ is _____—that's my _____. (guess, guest; hairy, Harry)

8. The workmen, who were totally _____, _____ on ladders as they used _____ material on the _____. (ceiling, sealing; staid, stayed)

9. _____-mannered, the _____ followed a _____ that ran along the _____. (boarder, border; coarse, course)

10. _____ unlikely that this essay—which states _____ point clearly and makes very good _____—will fail. (its, it's; sense, since)

SEQUENCE M EXERCISES

M·1   air, heir; made, maid
M·2   been, bin; flour, flower
M·3   its, it's; local, locale
M·4   hair, hare; tail, tale
M·5   lead, led; steal, steel
M·6   heard, herd; forth, fourth
M·7   retch, wretch; rye, wry
M·8   beat, beet; meat, meet
M·9   diner, dinner; desert, dessert
M·10 human, humane; gorilla, guerrilla

M·1

FOCUS   *Air:* the earth's atmosphere; a manner of doing something
Heir: an inheritor

Made: created; brought about
Maid: an unmarried woman; a female servant

STUDY   The maid was heir to a fortune.
The fortune was made by bottling air.
The air was mountain-fresh.

WRITE   The _____

that _____.

CHECK   A fortune had been _____
by bottling mountain-fresh

_____, and the _____

was _____ to it.

M·2

FOCUS   *Been:* a past form of the verb *be*
Bin: box for storing grain

Flour: ground grain
Flower: a blossom

STUDY   The cook had been scooping flour.
The flour was in the bin.
His wife handed him a flower.

WRITE   The _____

when _____.

74

CHECK The cook's wife handed a

_____ to the cook, who

had _____ scooping

_____ in the _____.

M•3

FOCUS   *Its:* belonging to it
      It's: it is

      Local: related to a small area
      Locale: location, area
STUDY   It's certainly a local interest
story.
The army will test its weapons.
The testing will be in this locale.

WRITE   _____

      that _____

_____.

CHECK   The fact that the army will

test _____ weapons in this

_____ is certainly a

_____ interest story.

M•4

FOCUS   *Hair:* a threadlike growth
from skin
      Hare: a rabbit

      Tail: the hind part
      Tale: a story
STUDY   The tale was hardly hair-
raising.
The tale concerned a hapless
hare.
The hare froze its tail in the ice.

WRITE   The _____

      that _____

      was _____.

CHECK   It was hardly _____-

raising—this _____ about

a hapless _____ that froze

its _____ in the ice.

M•5

FOCUS   *Lead:* a metal
      Led: guided

      Steal: to thieve
      Steel: metal
STUDY   Police were led to a junkyard.
Thieves were trying to steal lead
ingots.
Thieves were trying to steal sheet
steel.

WRITE   Police _____

      where _____

      and _____.
CHECK   In a junkyard, to which po-

lice were _____, thieves

were trying to _____ not

only _____ ingots but also

sheet _____.

M•6

FOCUS   *Heard:* listened to
      Herd: a large number of ani-
mals; to drive or direct a large
number of animals

Forth: forward, onward
Fourth: following the third

STUDY   Something happened on the fourth of June.
The herd finally broke forth.
The herd was heard by the townspeople.

WRITE   On _____, _____

_____ townspeople.

CHECK   It was on the _____ of June that the townspeople

_____ the _____,

which finally broke _____.

M•7

FOCUS   *Retch:* to vomit
Wretch: a miserable person

Rye: a type of grain
Wry: crooked

STUDY   The old wretch began to retch.
The old wretch was wry.
He had a fondness for rye whiskey.

WRITE   The _____, _____

_____, began _____.

CHECK   Because of his fondness for

_____ whiskey, the _____

old _____ began to _____.

M•8

FOCUS   *Beat:* to strike; to defeat
Beet: a vegetable

Meat: food, flesh of animals
Meet: to come upon; encounter; to come together (used here as a noun)

STUDY   There was a track meet.
The meat cutters beat competing workers.
The workers were from the sugar beet factory.

WRITE   There _____

where _____

from _____.

CHECK   The _____ cutters

_____ competing workers

from the sugar _____ factory at a track _____.

M•9

FOCUS   *Diner:* a roadside restaurant
Dinner: a main meal

Desert: to abandon; a dry piece of land
Dessert: last course of a meal

STUDY   Our dinner was served in the diner.
Our dessert was served in the diner.
The diner was located in the desert.

WRITE   Our _____;

it _____.

CHECK   The _____, where our

_____ and _____ were served, was located in the

_____.

M•10

FOCUS *Human:* like or belonging
to a human being
Humane: kind, merciful

Gorilla: a giant ape
Guerrilla: a voluntary (unoffi-
cial) soldier

STUDY The guerrilla was less than
humane.
He looked like a gorilla.

The gorilla had a human face.

WRITE The _____, _____

_____,

was _____.

CHECK Looking like a _____

—except for a _____

face—the _____ was less

than _____.

MASTERY QUIZ M

To demonstrate your mastery of words in Sequence M exercises, write out the following sentences in your own notebook, with the correct words filled in. (Do not check back to the exercises for definitions.)

1. The bottling of mountain-fresh _____ had _____ a fortune—and the _____ was _____ to it. (air, heir; made, maid)

2. The cook's wife handed a _____ to the cook, who had _____ scooping _____ in the _____. (been, bin; flour, flower)

3. The army's testing of _____ weapons in this _____ is certainly a _____ interest story. (its, it's; local, locale)

4. The _____ concerned a hapless _____ that froze its _____ in the ice; it was hardly _____-raising. (hair, hare; tail, tale)

5. Thieves were trying to _____ _____ ingots and sheet _____ in a junkyard to which police were _____. (lead, led; steal, steel)

6. The townspeople _____ the _____ that finally broke _____ on the _____ of June. (heard, herd; forth, fourth)

7. A fondness for _____ whiskey caused the _____ old _____ to _____. (retch, wretch; rye, wry)

8. At a track _____, the _____ cutters _____ competing workers from the sugar _____ factory. (beat, beet; meat, meet)

9. In the _____, located in the _____, our _____ and _____ were served. (diner, dinner; desert, dessert)

10. Less than _____, the _____ looked like a _____ with a _____ face. (human, humane; gorilla, guerrilla)

SEQUENCE N EXERCISES

N•1   sense, since; quiet, quite
N•2   leased, least; loan, lone
N•3   lessen, lesson; taught, taut
N•4   cellar, seller; pleas, please
N•5   mail, male; who's, whose
N•6   biding, bidding; peer, pier
N•7   ate, eight; sole, soul
N•8   lead, led; mind, mine
N•9   affect, effect; than, then
N•10 flaunt, flout; prince, prints

N•1

FOCUS   *Sense:* to feel or perceive; something that is reasonable
Since: connector meaning "because" or expressing time

Quiet: silent
Quite: truly, completely, entirely

STUDY   I sense something.
You're rather nervous.
It's quite quiet.

WRITE   I _____

_____.

CHECK   _____ it's _____

_____, I _____ that
you're rather nervous.

N•2

FOCUS   *Leased:* rented
Least: smallest

Loan: borrowed money
Lone: single; solitary

STUDY   The lone burglar had not the least guilt.
The burglar often leased his equipment.
He took out a business loan.

WRITE   _____, who _____

_____, had not _____

as _____.

CHECK   Taking out a business

_____, the _____

burglar—who often _____
his equipment—had not the

_____ guilt.

N•3

FOCUS   *Lessen:* to diminish
Lesson: an assignment to be studied

79

Taught: instructed
Taut: tight

STUDY I made efforts to lessen my fear.
My stomach still felt taut.
I taught my first lesson.

WRITE I _____;

however, _____

as _____.

CHECK In spite of efforts to _____
my fear, my stomach still felt

_____ as I _____ my

first _____.

N•4

FOCUS *Cellar:* a room under a house
Seller: one who sells

Pleas: arguments
Please: to delight; a polite addition to requests

STUDY We asked the seller please to reconsider.
She finally listened to our pleas.
We made our pleas in the cellar.

WRITE We _____,

and _____,

which _____.

CHECK In the _____ we made

our _____, asking the

_____ _____ to reconsider, which she finally did.

N•5

FOCUS *Mail:* letters, packages; flexible armor
Male: of the masculine sex; a man

Who's: who is
Whose: belonging to what person

STUDY Our mail carrier is a male chauvinist.
The carrier is about to be fired.
His reputation is notorious.

WRITE Our _____, _____,

is a _____

_____ notorious.

CHECK Our _____ carrier,

_____ reputation as a

_____ chauvinist is notorious, is about to be fired.

N•6

FOCUS *Biding:* staying, waiting
Bidding: offering of money

Peer: someone on an equal level
Pier: a wharf, boat dock

STUDY Joel had been biding his time.
He was playing poker on the pier.
A peer decided to up the bidding.

WRITE Joel _____,

playing _____,

when _____.

CHECK Playing poker on the

_____, Joel had been

_____ his time; then a

_____ decided to up the

_____.

N•7

FOCUS *Ate:* consumed
Eight: a number

Sole: part of a foot or shoe; only; type of fish
Soul: a human spirit; pertaining to black culture

STUDY I was the sole person at the table.
I regard sole as "soul food."
I ate eight helpings.

WRITE Because _____

and _____,

_____.

CHECK I _____ _____ help-

ings of _____—which I

regard as "_____ food"—

since I was the _____
person at the table.

N•8

FOCUS *Lead:* a metal
Led: guided toward

Mind: brain, thoughts
Mine: belonging to me; a large excavation, pit

STUDY I didn't mind something.
I was led to the lead mine.
The lead mine was now all mine.

WRITE I _____,

which _____.

CHECK The _____ _____

was now all _____ so I

didn't _____ being _____
to it.

N•9

FOCUS *Affect:* to influence (used here as a verb)
Effect: result (used here as a noun)

Than: introduces second element in a comparison
Then: at that time

STUDY A radiation effect began to affect health.
The radiation effect was greater than expected.
Then a public outcry arose from workers.

WRITE A _____

began _____,

and _____.

CHECK It was _____—after a

radiation _____ that was

greater _____ expected

began to _____ health—
that a public outcry arose from
workers.

N•10

FOCUS   *Flaunt:* to make a showy
display of
Flout: to show scorn for

Prince: a king's son
Prints: impressions or pictures
(noun); publishes (verb)

STUDY   The prince flaunted his art
prints.
His attempt was to make others
jealous.
He thereby flouted good manners.

WRITE   The _____

in _____

and _____.

CHECK   In an attempt to make others jealous, the _____

_____ his art _____

and thereby _____ good
manners.

MASTERY QUIZ N

To demonstrate your mastery of words in Sequence N exercises, write out the following sentences in your own notebook, with the correct words filled in. (Do not check back to the exercises for definitions.)

1. My _____ is that you're rather nervous, _____ it's _____ _____. (since, sense; quiet, quite)

2. The _____ burglar often _____ his equipment; he had not the _____ guilt as he took out a business _____. (leased, least; loan, lone)

3. Although I made efforts to _____ my fear, my stomach still felt _____ as I _____ my first _____. (lessen, lesson; taught, taut)

4. After we asked her _____ to reconsider, the _____ finally listened to our _____ in the _____. (cellar, seller; pleas, please)

5. About to be fired, our _____ carrier is a _____ chauvinist _____ reputation is notorious. (mail, male; who's, whose)

6. _____ his time, Joel was playing poker on the _____ until a _____ decided to up the _____. (biding, bidding; peer, pier)

7. The _____ person at the table, I _____ _____ helpings of _____, which I regard as "_____ food." (ate, eight; sole, soul)

8. Now that the _____ _____ was all _____, I didn't _____ being _____ to it. (lead, led; mind, mine)

9. A greater _____ expected radiation _____ began to _____ health; _____ a public outcry arose from workers. (affect, effect; than, then)

10. _____ good manners, the _____ attempted to make others jealous by _____ his art _____. (flaunting, flouting; prince, prints)

SEQUENCE O EXERCISES

O·1   find, fined; their, they're
O·2   your, you're; meat, meet
O·3   one, won; son, sun
O·4   pair, pear; scene, seen
O·5   which, witch; wear, where
O·6   liar, lyre; base, bass
O·7   pause, paws; bare, bear
O·8   prince, prints; throne, thrown
O·9   holy, wholly; capital, capitol
O·10   altar, alter; presence, presents

O·1

FOCUS   *Find:* to locate
Fined: financially penalized

Their: belonging to them
They're: they are

STUDY   They're sure to get fined.
They couldn't find their library books.
The books are overdue.

WRITE   _____

because _____.

CHECK   They couldn't _____

_____ overdue library

books; therefore, _____

sure to get _____.

O·2

FOCUS   *Your:* belonging to you
You're: you are

Meat: food, flesh of animals
Meet: to come upon, encounter; to come together

STUDY   You're having trouble "making ends meet."
You may have to give up meat.
The meat is in your food budget.

WRITE   If _____,

you _____.

CHECK   _____ trouble with

"making ends _____" may

mean that _____ going to

have to give up _____ in

_____ food budget.

O·3

FOCUS   *One:* a single unit; a certain person
Won: finished first; succeeded; gained

Son: a male child
Sun: the star that provides light and heat

STUDY His son was the one.
His son won the competition.
The competition was in sun bathing.

WRITE His _____

who _____.

CHECK In the _____-bathing

competition, his _____ was

the _____ who _____.

O·4

FOCUS Pair: two of a kind
Pear: a fruit

Scene: a sight; part of a play
Seen: observed

STUDY We've seen the pair.
The pair created a scene.
The pair shared a pear.

WRITE We've _____

who _____

by _____.

CHECK The _____ who cre-

ated a _____ by sharing a

_____ have been _____.

O·5

FOCUS Which: what one of several
Witch: a practicer of magic; an old, ugly woman

Wear: to carry on one's body; to weaken, harass
Where: in or at what place

STUDY Our teacher may be a witch.
Her temper often wears thin.

She knows which words go where.

WRITE Although _____

whose _____,

she _____.

CHECK Our teacher, whose temper

often _____ thin, may be

a _____; nevertheless, she

knows _____ words go

_____.

O•6

FOCUS *Liar:* falsifier, one who lies
Lyre: musical instrument

Base: mean; the foundation of an object
Bass: musical term; deep

STUDY The convict began to strum the lyre.
The convict began to sing in a bass voice.
The convict was a base liar.

WRITE The convict, a _____,

began _____

and _____.

CHECK A _____ _____,
the convict began to strum the

_____, singing in a

_____ voice.

O•7

FOCUS *Pause:* to stop momentarily
Paws: an animal's feet

Bare: naked
Bear: an animal; to carry

STUDY We'll pause to consider the paws.
The paws are the bear's.
The paws have been shaved bare.

WRITE We'll _____

that _____.

CHECK The _____'s _____,

shaved _____, are what

we'll _____ to consider.

O•8

FOCUS *Prince:* a king's son
Prints: impressions or pictures (noun); publishes (verb)

Throne: the seat of a king
Thrown: hurled

STUDY The prince gave up his throne.
His art prints were thrown away.
His art prints were deeply treasured.

WRITE After _____,

his _____.

CHECK Deeply treasured art _____

that the _____ owned were

_____ away when he gave

up his _____.

O•9

FOCUS *Holy:* pure, sacred
Wholly: completely, fully

Capital: principal; punishable by death
Capitol: statehouse

STUDY We were wholly unprepared for one fact.
Capital crimes were common in the capitol.
The capitol was supposedly quite holy.

WRITE _____ for the fact that

_____,

which was _____.

CHECK That _____ crimes

were common in the _____,
which was supposedly quite

_____, was a fact for which

we were _____ unprepared.

O•10

FOCUS *Altar:* a platform for sacrifices
Alter: to change

Presence: being present
Presents: gifts

STUDY The presence did not alter anything.
The presence was of your presents.
The presents were on the altar.

WRITE The _____

_____ anything.

CHECK Your _____ were on

the _____; however, their

_____ did not _____

anything.

MASTERY QUIZ O

To demonstrate your mastery of words in Sequence O exercises, write out the following sentences in your own notebook, with the correct words filled in. (Do not check back to the exercises for definitions.)

1. Because they couldn't _____ _____ overdue library books, _____ sure to get _____. (find, fined; their, they're)

2. Give up _____ in _____ food budget if _____ having trouble "making ends _____." (your, you're; meat, meet)

3. The _____ who _____ the competition in _____-bathing was his _____. (one, won; son, sun)

4. We've _____ the _____; they created a _____ by sharing a _____. (pair, pear; scene, seen)

5. Our teacher may be a _____ whose temper often _____ thin, but she knows _____ words go _____. (which, witch; wears, where)

6. The convict was a _____ _____; nevertheless, he began to strum the _____ and sing in a _____ voice. (liar, lyre; base, bass)

7. The _____'s _____ have been shaved _____; let's _____ to consider them. (pause, paws; bare, bear)

8. The _____ gave up his _____; then his art _____, which were deeply treasured, were _____ away. (prince, prints; throne, thrown)

9. Since the _____ was supposedly quite _____, we were _____ unprepared to find that _____ crimes were common. (holy, wholly; capital, capitol)

10. Your _____ on the _____ did not _____ anything. (altar, alter; presence, presents)

SEQUENCE P EXERCISES

P•1   I'll, isle; hear, here
P•2   gilt, guilt; knight, night
P•3   him, hymn; higher, hire
P•4   aid, aide; formally, formerly
P•5   are, our; elicit, illicit
P•6   leans, liens; loan, lone
P•7   all ready, already; which, witch
P•8   one, won; knot, not
P•9   laid, lain; lay, lie
P•10   cereal, serial; correspondence, correspondents

P•1

FOCUS   *I'll:* I will
        Isle: an island

        Hear: to listen to
        Here: in this place
STUDY   I'll remain on the isle.
        You'll have to sit here.
        You'll have to hear me out.

WRITE _____,

but _____

and _____.

CHECK _____ remain on the

_____; however, you'll not

only have to sit _____ but

you'll also have to _____
me out.

P•2

FOCUS   *Gilt:* golden
        Guilt: shame

        Knight: a title of honor
        Night: darkness
STUDY   The knight wore a gilt-col-
        ored cloak.
        He slipped unnoticed into the
        night.
        He felt no trace of guilt.

WRITE   Wearing _____,

the _____,

feeling _____.

CHECK   Unnoticed in spite of his

_____-colored cloak, the

_____ slipped into the

_____ and felt no trace of

_____.

89

P•3

FOCUS   *Him:* that man
Hymn: a sacred song

Higher: farther up; more acute in pitch
Hire: to employ

STUDY   We wanted to hire him.
His job would be to sing a hymn.
We needed a higher voice.

WRITE   Although _____

_____,

we _____.

CHECK   We wanted to _____

_____ to sing a _____;
however, we needed a

_____ voice.

P•4

FOCUS   *Aid:* help (used here as a noun)
Aide: helper

Formally: correctly; in a dignified way
Formerly: earlier

STUDY   The aide formerly wore jeans.
He must now dress more formally.
He teaches a first-aid class.

WRITE   Although _____,

he _____

because _____.

CHECK   The _____ teaching a

first-_____ class _____
wore jeans but now must dress

more _____.

P•5

FOCUS   *Are:* present tense of *be*
Our: belonging to us

Elicit: to draw forth, evoke
Illicit: unlawful

STUDY   Our questions are guaranteed to elicit a confession.
Our questions are accompanied by violence.
The confession is about illicit drug traffic.

WRITE   _____,

when _____,

_____ traffic.

CHECK   When _____ ques-

tions _____ accompanied by

violence, they _____ guar-

anteed to _____ a confes-

sion about _____ drug traffic.

P•6

FOCUS   *Leans:* bends or slants
Liens: mortgages

Loan: borrowed money
Lone: solitary

STUDY   The bank's loan arranger leans back.
The loan arranger is lone.
She thinks about her many liens.

WRITE As _____,

she _____.

CHECK Thinking about her many

_____, the bank's _____

_____ arranger _____

back.

P•7

FOCUS *All ready:* prepared
Already: by or before given time

Which: what one of several
Witch: a practicer of magic; an old, ugly woman

STUDY The witches are already in costume.
They are all ready to be auditioned.
One wonders which to choose first.

WRITE The _____

and _____;

one _____.

CHECK One wonders _____

_____ to choose first when

they are _____ in cos-

tume, _____ to be audi-

tioned.

P•8

FOCUS *One:* a single unit; a certain person

Won: finished first; succeeded; gained

Knot: a cord or rope tied
Not: a word used to express the negative

STUDY One person was not announced.
The person won the contest.
The contest was in knot-tying.

WRITE _____, who _____

_____, was _____.

CHECK The person who was

_____ announced was the

_____ who _____ the

_____-tying contest.

P•9

FOCUS *Laid:* placed; set forth
Lain: rested, been stored away

Lay: reclined, rested
Lie: a falsehood, untruth (noun); to utter a falsehood (verb); to rest (verb)

STUDY She lay on the floor.
She laid out the lie.
The lie had lain in her heart.

WRITE As _____,

she _____

that _____.

CHECK The _____ that had

_____ in her heart was

_____ out as she _____

on the floor.

P•10

FOCUS *Cereal:* a breakfast food
      Serial: appearing in installments

      Correspondence: exchange of letters
      Correspondents: people who write; journalists

STUDY Company correspondence indicates something.
      A TV serial will sell breakfast cereal.

      The serial features news correspondents.

WRITE Company _____
      that _____
      if it _____.

CHECK According to company
      _____, breakfast
      _____ can be sold by a
      TV _____ that features
      news _____.

MASTERY QUIZ P

To demonstrate your mastery of words in Sequence P exercises, write out the following sentences in your own notebook, with the correct words filled in. (Do not check back to the exercises for definitions.)

1. If you'll sit _____ and _____ me out, _____ remain on the _____. (I'll, isle; hear, here)

2. The _____ wore a _____-colored cloak, slipped unnoticed into the _____, and felt no trace of _____. (gilt, guilt; knight, night)

3. We wanted to _____ _____, but a _____ voice was needed to sing a _____. (him, hymn; higher, hire)

4. _____ the _____ teaching a first-_____ class wore jeans; now, however, he must dress more _____. (aid, aide; formally, formerly)

5. _____ questions _____ accompanied by violence; they _____ guaranteed to _____ a confession about _____ drug traffic. (are, our; elicit, illicit)

6. With thoughts about her many _____, the bank's _____ _____ arranger _____ back. (leans, liens; loan, lone)

7. With the _____ _____ in costume and _____ to be auditioned, one wonders _____ to choose first. (all ready, already; which, witches)

8. The contest in _____-tying was _____ by _____ person who was _____ announced. (one, won; knot, not)

9. A _____ had _____ in her heart; she _____ it out as she _____ on the floor. (laid, lain; lay, lie)

10. A TV _____ will sell breakfast _____ if it features news _____—this according to company _____. (cereal, serial; correspondence, correspondents)

SEQUENCE Q EXERCISES

Q·1   sighs, size; wait, weight
Q·2   aisle, isle; bridal, bridle
Q·3   days, daze; meat, meet
Q·4   tense, tents; weak, week
Q·5   peace, piece; peak, peek
Q·6   accept, except; guessed, guest
Q·7   son, sun; threw, through
Q·8   affect, effect; miner, minor
Q·9   caught, cot; colonel, kernel
Q·10   dairy, diary; riding, writing

Q·1

FOCUS *Sighs:* long, deep, audible breaths
Size: dimension or magnitude

Wait: to stay for, remain; to pause
Weight: heaviness; a heavy object

STUDY The lifter waits for the right moment.
He grips the weights.
He eyes their size.
He sighs in protest.

WRITE The _____,

_____, _____,

and _____.

CHECK The lifter, gripping the

_____ and eyeing their

_____, _____ for the

right moment and _____
in protest.

Q·2

FOCUS *Aisle:* a narrow passageway
Isle: an island

Bridal: related to a wedding (bride)
Bridle: part of a harness; to restrain

STUDY Mona ran down the aisle.
She threw off her bridal veil.
She fitted her horse's bridle.
She rode angrily across the isle.

WRITE Mona _____,

_____,

_____,

and _____.

CHECK After running down the

_____, throwing off her

_____ veil, and fitting her

horse's _____, Mona rode

angrily across the _____.

94

Q•3

FOCUS   *Days:* a period of time
Daze: a stunned, bewildered condition

Meat: food, flesh of animals
Meet: to come upon, encounter; to come together
STUDY   I wanted to meet Pete.
He's been in a daze.
The daze has lasted for days.
He failed a course in meat cutting.

WRITE   I _____,

but _____

that _____

because _____.
CHECK   Pete, whom I wanted to

_____, has been in a

_____ for _____ be-

cause he failed a _____-cutting course.

Q•4

FOCUS   *Tense:* taut; ill-at-ease
Tents: portable canvas shelters

Weak: lacking strength
Week: seven days
STUDY   The protesters lived for a week.
They lived in tents.
They then began to grow tense.
They then began to grow weak.

WRITE   The _____

and then _____.

CHECK   After living for a _____

in _____, the protesters

grew _____ and _____.

Q•5

FOCUS   *Peace:* quiet
Piece: a part of something

Peak: the highest point
Peek: to look quickly
STUDY   A piece of sun began to peek through.
The peeking was through cloud cover.
The expedition reached the mountain's peak.
The world seemed completely at peace there.

WRITE   A _____

just as _____,

where _____.
CHECK   The expedition reached the

mountain's _____, where
the world seemed completely

at _____, with a _____

of sun beginning to _____
through cloud cover.

Q•6

FOCUS   *Accept:* to receive, to approve
Except: to leave out or take out

Guessed: speculated about
Guest: a visitor

STUDY Our hostess was ready to accept the thief.
The thief was disguised as a guest.
This was except for one fact.
Someone guessed his real purpose.

WRITE Our _____

who _____—

_____.

CHECK The thief was disguised as

a _____, and our hostess

was ready to _____ him—

_____ that someone _____

his real purpose.

Q•7

FOCUS *Son:* a male child
Sun: the star that provides light and heat

Threw: hurled
Through: in one side, out the other; finished

STUDY The sun blazed down on the arena.
The manager reluctantly threw in the towel.
This signaled something to the referee.
His son was through fighting.

WRITE As _____,

the _____,

signaling _____

_____.

CHECK As he reluctantly _____

in the towel, with the _____ blazing down on the arena, the manager signaled to the ref-

eree that his _____ was

_____ fighting.

Q•8

FOCUS *Affect:* to influence (used here as a verb)
Effect: to carry out, cause to happen (used here as a verb)

Miner: a worker in a mine
Minor: one who is underage; musical term; insignificant

STUDY We hope to effect a pension plan.
The plan will positively affect miners.
Miners now have coverage.
The coverage is only minor.

WRITE We _____

that _____,

who _____.

CHECK In an effort to _____

_____ positively—they now

have only _____ cover-

age—we hope to _____

a pension plan.

Q•9

FOCUS *Caught:* seized and held
Cot: a narrow bed

Colonel: a military officer
Kernel: a grain or seed

STUDY   The colonel was caught.
He was lying on his cot.
He was eating sunflower kernels.
The kernels were smuggled.

WRITE   The _____,

eating _____.

CHECK _____ lying   on   his

_____, the _____ was
eating   smuggled   sunflower

_____.

Q·10

FOCUS   *Dairy:* milk-producing farm
Diary: a written record of one's
experiences

Riding: being   carried—as   on
horseback
Writing: forming letters, words,
sentences

STUDY   Juan wanted to go bareback
riding.
The riding was at the dairy.
Marty was intent on writing.
The writing was in his diary.

WRITE   Juan _____,

but _____.

CHECK   What Juan wanted was to

go _____ bareback   at   the

_____;   however,   Marty

was intently _____ in his

_____.

MASTERY QUIZ Q

To demonstrate your mastery of words in Sequence Q exercises, write out
the following sentences in your own notebook, with the correct words
filled in. (Do not check back to the exercises for definitions.)

1. Gripping the _____, eyeing their _____, the lifter _____

for the right moment and _____ in protest. (sighs, size; waits,
weights)

2. Mona ran down the _____ and threw off her _____ veil;

then she fitted her horse's _____ and rode angrily across the

_____. (aisle, isle; bridal, bridle)

3. I wanted to _____ Pete; however, his _____ has lasted

for _____ because he failed a course in _____ cutting.
(days, daze; meat, meet)

MASTERY QUIZ Q
CONTINUED

4. The protestors, living for a _____ in _____, began to grow _____ and _____. (tense, tents; weak, week)

5. The world seemed completely at _____ when the expedition reached the mountain's _____, and a _____ of sun began to _____ through cloud cover. (peace, piece; peak, peek)

6. _____ for the fact that someone _____ the identity of the thief disguised as a _____, our hostess was ready to _____ him. (accept, except; guessed, guest)

7. The _____ blazed down on the arena; signaling to the referee that his _____ was _____ fighting, the manager reluctantly _____ in the towel. (son, sun; threw, through)

8. Our hope is to _____ a pension plan to _____ _____ positively since they now have only _____ coverage. (affect, effect; miners, minor)

9. Smuggled sunflower _____ were being eaten by the _____, who was _____ lying on his _____. (caught, cot; colonel, kernels)

10. Although Juan wanted to go bareback _____ at the _____, Marty was intent on _____ in his _____. (dairy, diary; riding, writing)

SEQUENCE R EXERCISES

R•1 mail, male; sail, sale
R•2 fir, fur; grisly, grizzly
R•3 knew, new; its, it's
R•4 knight, night; root, route
R•5 sole, soul; weak, week
R•6 decent, dissent; censor, censure
R•7 ascent, assent; climb, clime
R•8 well, we'll; picture, pitcher
R•9 cite, sight; their, they're
R•10 advice, advise; affect, effect

R•1

FOCUS *Mail:* letters, packages, flexible armor
Male: of the masculine sex; a man

Sail: the canvas of a boat or ship; to travel in a boat or ship
Sale: to be sold

STUDY John was a male.
He wanted to sail.
He found a boat on sale.
He ordered it through the mail.

WRITE Since _____

who _____,

he _____

and _____.

CHECK John, a _____ who

wanted to _____, found a

boat on _____ and or-

dered it through the _____.

R•2

FOCUS *Fir:* an evergreen tree
Fur: soft hair covering animal

Grisly: frightful
Grizzly: a bear; gray

STUDY We sat on a fir log.
We stared at a grisly sight.
The sight was a grizzly.
Its fur was stained with blood.

WRITE We _____,

staring _____:

a _____.

CHECK Sitting on a _____ log,

we stared at a _____ and

99

its bloodstained _____—a

_____ sight.

R·3

FOCUS *Knew:* perceived or under-
stood
New: fresh or unused

Its: belonging to it
It's: it is
STUDY The company already knew
something.
It's tough to sell a product.
The product is new.
Its name is unknown.

WRITE The _____

_____

when _____.
CHECK The   company   already

_____ that, when _____

name is unknown, _____

tough to sell a _____
product.

R·4

FOCUS *Knight:* a title of honor
Night: darkness

Root: part of a plant; the source,
essential part
Route: road, pathway
STUDY The knight took a route.

The route was unsafe at night.
He searched for a root.
The root was medicinal.

WRITE The _____

that _____

as _____.

CHECK Taking a _____ that

was unsafe at _____, the

_____ searched for a

_____ that was medicinal.

R•5

FOCUS *Sole:* part of a foot or shoe;
only; type of fish
Soul: human spirit; pertaining
to black culture

Weak: lacking strength
Week: seven days

STUDY Something happened in less
than a week.
The shoemaker grew weak.
He sold his soul to the devil.
He wanted to be sole owner of
the shop.

WRITE In _____,

the _____

and _____

because _____.

CHECK It was because the shoe-

maker wanted to be _____

owner of a shop in less than

a _____ that he grew

_____ and sold his

_____ to the devil.

R•6

FOCUS *Decent:* correct, right, proper
Dissent: to disagree with, protest (used here as a noun)

Censor: an official with power
to prohibit
Censure: to disapprove strongly
of, condemn

STUDY The group tried to censor
textbooks.
The group tried to censure
teachers.
The group's name was "Decent
Folks."
It used vocal dissent.

WRITE _____, whose name

was _____,

tried _____

_____.

CHECK Through vocal _____,

an attempt was made by a group

named "_____ Folks" to

_____ textbooks and

_____ teachers.

R•7

FOCUS *Ascent:* an upward climb
or movement
Assent: agreement or consent
(used here as a noun)

Climb: to ascend gradually
Clime: climate

STUDY Getting his assent was one
thing.

The assent was to make the ascent.
Making the climb would be something else.
The climb was into a freezing clime.

WRITE Getting _____

_____ ;

but making _____

_____ .

CHECK While getting his _____

to make the _____ would be one thing, it would be some-

thing else to make the _____

into a freezing _____ .

R•8

FOCUS *Well:* in a good manner; a hole in the ground
We'll: we will

Picture: a likeness of some-thing—a photograph or painting
Pitcher: a container for liquids; a baseball player
STUDY Will looked at the picture.
Will was a baseball pitcher.
The picture was a wishing well.
He said, "We'll draw it equally well."

WRITE _____ , _____ ,

looked _____ ,

saying _____ .

CHECK After looking at the _____

of the wishing _____ , a

baseball _____ named Will

said, "_____ draw it

equally _____ ."

R•9

FOCUS *Cite:* to quote or mention as an example; to summon be-fore a court
Site: a location or scene

Their: belonging to them
They're: they are
STUDY I'll cite their decision.
Their decision is to find a site.
The site is for building.
They're nearly bankrupt.

WRITE I'll _____

_____

even though _____ .

CHECK _____ decision to find

a building _____—in

spite of the fact _____ nearly bankrupt—is what I'll

_____ .

R•10

FOCUS *Advice:* counsel (a noun)
Advise: to give advice to (a verb)

Affect: to influence (used here as a verb)
Effect: result (used here as a noun)
STUDY We continue to advise our clients.

We continue to affect their decisions.
The decisions are on investments.
The overall effect of our advice is unknown.

WRITE   We _____

and _____,

but _____.

CHECK   While we continue to

_____ our clients and to

_____ their investment de-

cisions, the overall _____

of our _____ is unknown.

MASTERY QUIZ R

To demonstrate your mastery of words in Sequence R exercises, write out the following sentences in your own notebook, with the correct words filled in. (Do not check back to the exercises for definitions.)

1. A _____ named John wanted to _____; he found a boat on _____ and ordered it through the _____. (mail, male; sail, sale)

2. Staring at a _____ sight—a _____ with bloodstained _____—we sat on a _____ log. (fir, fur; grisly, grizzly)

3. A _____ product is tough to sell, the company _____, if _____ name is unknown. (knew, new; its, it's)

4. Searching for a medicinal _____, the _____ took a _____ that was unsafe at _____. (knight, night; root, route)

5. The shoemaker, growing _____ in less than a _____ because he wanted to be _____ owner of the shop, sold his _____ to the devil. (sole, soul; weak, week)

6. In an attempt to _____ textbooks and _____ teachers, a group named "_____ Folks" used vocal _____. (decent, dissent; censor, censure)

7. It would be one thing to get his _____ to making the _____ but something else to make the _____ into a freezing _____. (ascent, assent; climb, clime)

8. "_____ draw it equally _____," said Will, a baseball _____, as he looked at the _____ of the wishing _____. (well, we'll; picture, pitcher)

9. It's because _____ nearly bankrupt that I'll _____ _____ decision to find a building _____. (cite, site; their, they're)

10. The overall _____ of our _____ is unknown; however, we continue to _____ our clients and _____ their investment decisions. (advice, advise; affect, effect)

SEQUENCE S
EXERCISES

S•1 stairs, stares; suite, sweet
S•2 tide, tied; wait, weight
S•3 residence, residents; staid, stayed
S•4 air, heir; ascent, assent
S•5 riding, writing; stationary, stationery
S•6 close, clothes; formal, former
S•7 acts, ax(e); vice, vise
S•8 parish, perish; weak, week
S•9 moral, morale; personal, personnel
S•10 alley, ally; emigrate, immigrate

S•1

FOCUS *Stairs:* a flight of steps
Stares: gazes (used here as a verb)

Suite: a hotel room
Sweet: luscious, fragrant, pleasing

STUDY She climbs the stairs.
The stairs lead to her suite.
She stares out at the city's lights.
She thinks, "Sweet success!"

WRITE After climbing _____

_____,

she _____

and _____.

CHECK What she thinks—after she

climbs the _____ that

lead to her _____ and

_____ out at the city's

lights—is, "_____ success!"

S•2

FOCUS *Tide:* rise and fall of the ocean
Tied: bound with string or rope

Wait: to stay for, remain; to pause
Weight: heaviness, a heavy object

STUDY The tide washed in.
The prisoner could only wait.
He thought about the weight.
It was tied to his ankles.

WRITE As _____,

the _____,

thinking _____

that _____.

CHECK In washed the _____,
but the prisoner could only

_____, thinking about the

_____ that was _____
to his ankles.

S·3

FOCUS *Residence:* the place one
lives
Residents: people who live in a
place

Staid: sober, solemn, quiet
Stayed: remained
STUDY The residents stayed for the
rally.
The residents were staid.
The rally protested rent increases.
Increases were for their place of
residence.

WRITE The _____

that _____

for _____.
CHECK Protesting rent increases for

their place of _____,

the _____ _____

_____ for the rally.

S·4

FOCUS *Air:* the earth's atmosphere; a manner of doing
something
Heir: an inheritor

Ascent: an upward climb or
movement

Assent: agreement or consent
(used here as a noun)
STUDY The heir made her ascent.
The ascent was to the throne.
The ascent was with an air of
grace.
The ascent was with her mother's
assent.

WRITE The _____

with _____

and _____.

CHECK The _____—with an

_____ of grace and her

mother's _____—made her

_____ to the throne.

S·5

FOCUS *Riding:* being carried—as
on horseback
Writing: forming letters, words,
etc.

Stationary: fixed, not moving
Stationery: writing materials
STUDY I went riding.
Tonya remained stationary.
She was writing on her sta-
tionery.
The stationery was personalized.

WRITE While _____,

Tonya _____,

_____.

CHECK Tonya remained _____,

_____ on her personal-

ized _____; however, I

went _____.

S•6

FOCUS *Close:* to shut, bring to an
end
Clothes: wearing apparel

Formal: correct, dignified
Former: preceding, earlier; the
first of two

STUDY My tailor decided to close
his store.
The tailor was my former one.
The store sold clothes.
The clothes were formal.

WRITE My _____,

which sold _____.

CHECK _____ _____

were sold by my _____ tailor in his store, but he decided

to _____ it.

S•7

FOCUS *Acts:* behavior
Ax(e): a tool for chopping

Vice: an evil action or habit
Vise: a device to hold objects
firmly

STUDY The ax(e) was once a tool.
The vise was once a tool.
The tools were for reducing
vice.
The tools were for reducing
criminal acts.

WRITE The _____

for _____.

CHECK Reducing _____ and

criminal _____ was once

accomplished by means of tools

such as the _____ and

the _____.

S•8

FOCUS *Parish:* congregation of a
church
Perish: to be destroyed or ruined

Weak: lacking strength
Week: seven days

STUDY The priest spoke once a
week.
He reminded people in his
parish.
Their souls would surely perish.
Their will power was weak.

WRITE The _____,

reminding _____

that _____

if _____.

CHECK Speaking once a _____

to those in his _____, the
priest reminded people that if

their will power was _____,

their souls would surely _____.

S•9

FOCUS *Moral:* concerning right and
wrong
Morale: mental condition of a
person or group

Personal: private, individual
Personnel: persons employed at
work

STUDY A decline affects morale.
The decline is moral.
The morale is our personnel's.
The morale is personal.

WRITE A _____

_____.

CHECK Our _____'s _____

_____ is affected by a

_____ decline.

S·10

FOCUS *Alley:* a narrow thoroughfare
Ally: one who cooperates with another

Emigrate: to leave one's homeland for another country
Immigrate: to come into a country after leaving one's homeland

STUDY Two women crossed the alley simultaneously.
The women had once been allies.
One was immigrating into the United States.
One was emigrating from the United States.

WRITE Two _____

crossed _____—

one _____,

the other _____.

CHECK Crossing   the _____
simultaneously were two women   who   had   once   been

_____—one _____
into the United States, the other

_____ from   the   United States.

MASTERY QUIZ S

To demonstrate your mastery of words in Sequence S exercises, write out the following sentences in your own notebook, with the correct words filled in. (Do not check back to the exercises for definitions.)

1. She climbs the _____ that lead to her _____, _____ out at the city's lights, and thinks, "_____ success!" (stairs, stares; suite, sweet)

2. With the _____ washing in, the prisoner, thinking about the _____ _____ to his ankles, could only _____. (tide, tied; wait, weight)

3. To protest rent increases for their place of _____, the _____, who were _____, _____ for the rally. (residence, residents; staid, stayed)

4. With a graceful _____ and her mother's _____, the _____ made her _____ to the throne. (air, heir; ascent, assent)

5. Remaining _____, Tonya was _____ on her personalized _____ while I went _____. (riding, writing; stationary, stationery)

6. My _____ tailor sold _____ _____ in his store; however, he decided to _____ it. (close, clothes; formal, former)

7. Tools such as the _____ and the _____ were once used to reduce _____ and criminal _____. (acts, ax(e); vice, vise)

8. Once a _____ people in the _____ were reminded by the priest that their souls would surely _____ if their will power was _____. (parish, perish; weak, week)

9. The _____ _____ of our _____ is affected by a _____ decline. (moral, morale; personal, personnel)

10. Two women who had once been _____ crossed the _____; one was _____ from the United States, whereas the other was _____ into the United States. (alley, allies; emigrating, immigrating)

SEQUENCE T EXERCISES

T·1	altar, alter; allowed, aloud
T·2	beach, beech; creak, creek
T·3	bail, bale; marshal, martial
T·4	peace, piece; pray, prey
T·5	foreword, forward; currant, current
T·6	beats, beets; brews, bruise
T·7	formal, former; later, latter
T·8	imply, infer; lacks, lax
T·9	eminent, imminent; weather, whether
T·10	correspondence, correspondents; discreet, discrete

T·1

FOCUS   *Altar:* a platform for sacrifices
Alter: to change

Allowed: permitted
Aloud: not silently

STUDY   I can't alter the fact.
No one is allowed to sing.
The singing would be aloud.
The singing would be at the altar.

WRITE   I _____

that _____

_____

CHECK   The fact that no one is

_____ to sing _____

at the _____ is something I can't _____.

T·2

FOCUS   *Beach:* a sandy shore
Beech: a hardwood tree bearing nuts

Creak: a harsh, squeaking sound
Creek: a small stream

STUDY   I stood near a mossy creek.
It burbled toward the beach.
I heard trees creak.
The trees were beech.

WRITE   Standing _____

that _____,

I _____.

CHECK   I heard _____ trees

_____ as I stood near a

mossy _____ that burbled

toward the _____.

T•3

FOCUS   *Bail:* a deposit for release from jail
Bale: a large bundle

Marshal: a judicial or military officer
Martial: warlike, bold

STUDY   The marshal sat on a hay bale.
The marshal assumed an attitude.
The attitude was martial.
The thug posted bail.

WRITE   Sitting _____,

the _____

as _____.

CHECK   The _____, assuming

a _____ attitude, sat on

a hay _____ as the thug

posted _____.

T•4

FOCUS   *Peace:* quiet
Piece: a part of something

Pray: to petition (God); to offer a prayer
Prey: to hunt; to victimize

STUDY   A piece of the editorial is ironic.
It points out the fact.
Good people pray for peace.
Thieves prey on their cars.

WRITE   A _____

because _____

that while _____,

thieves _____.

CHECK   An ironic _____ of the

editorial is that thieves _____
on the cars of good people

while they _____ for

_____.

T•5

FOCUS   *Foreword:* a preface
Forward: onward, moving ahead; bold

Currant: a seedless raisin
Current: happening now

STUDY   Perhaps I'm being somewhat forward.
Let me criticize the book's foreword.
It ignores current approaches.
The approaches are for making currant jelly.

WRITE   Although _____,

let _____

because _____.

CHECK   I'm   being   somewhat

_____ perhaps, but let me

criticize the _____ of the

book: _____ approaches

for making _____ jelly are
ignored.

T•6

FOCUS   *Beats:* strikes, defeats
Beets: a vegetable

Brews: makes into beverage
Bruise: to injure, to crush
STUDY   He beats the beets.
He wants to bruise them.
He wants to mash them.
He brews the pulp into wine.

WRITE   First, _____

to _____;

then _____.

CHECK   After he _____ the

_____ to _____ and

mash them, he _____ the
pulp into wine.

T•7

STUDY   *Formal:* correct, dignified
Former: preceding, earlier; the
first of two

Later: afterward in time
Latter: the second of two
WRITE   Bill and Phil applied for the
job.
I at first liked the former.
The former presented a formal
image.
I later chose the latter candidate.

WRITE   When _____,

I _____

because he _____,

but _____.

CHECK   Bill and Phil applied for the
job; although I at first liked the

_____ image of the _____,

I _____ chose the _____
candidate.

T•8

FOCUS   *Imply:* to hint, suggest
Infer: to conclude by reasoning

Lacks: is deficient in, is without
Lax: loose, slack
STUDY   We infer something from
the discipline.
The discipline was extremely
lax.
Mr. Freeman lacks the ability to
teach.
Our report will not imply this.

WRITE   We _____

that _____,

but _____.

CHECK   Although we _____

from his extremely _____
discipline that Mr. Freeman

_____ the ability to teach,

our report will not _____
this.

T•9

FOCUS   *Eminent:* high in rank, distinguished
Imminent: impending

Weather: condition of the at-
mosphere
Whether: if (used here as a
connector)
STUDY   A scientist will discuss
something.
The scientist is eminent.
The weather change indicates
something.
A new Ice Age is imminent.

WRITE An _____

_____

that _____ .

CHECK _____ the _____
change indicates that a new Ice

Age is _____ will be dis-

cussed by an _____ scien-
tist.

T·10

FOCUS *Correspondence:* exchange
of letters
Correspondents: people who
write; journalists

Discreet: careful about what
one says
Discrete: separate and distinct
STUDY There was a correspondence.
The correspondence was dis-
creet.
It was between two lonely
correspondents.
They worked on discrete parts
of the newspaper.

WRITE There _____

between _____

who _____ .

CHECK Two lonely _____

who worked on _____
parts of the newspaper had a

_____ _____ .

MASTERY QUIZ T

To demonstrate your mastery of words in Sequence T exercises, write out the following sentences in your own notebook, with the correct words filled in. (Do not check back to the exercises for definitions.)

1. No one is _____ to sing _____ at the _____; that's a fact I can't _____. (altar, alter; allowed, aloud)

2. I stood near a mossy _____ that burbled toward the _____ and heard _____ trees _____. (beach, beech; creak, creek)

3. As the thug posted _____, the _____ sat on a hay _____ and assumed a _____ attitude. (bail, bale; marshal, martial)

4. The editorial has an ironic _____ that points out a fact: As good people _____ for _____, thieves _____ on their cars. (peace, piece; pray, prey)

5. To criticize the book's _____ is somewhat _____ of me, but it ignores _____ approaches for making _____ jelly. (foreword, forward; currant, current)

6. Before he _____ the pulp into wine, he _____ the _____ to _____ and crush them. (beats, beets; brews, bruise)

7. Of the two applicants, Bill and Phil, I at first liked the _____ image presented by the _____; _____, however, I chose the _____ candidate. (formal, former; later, latter)

8. From his extremely _____ discipline we _____ that Mr. Freeman _____ the ability to teach; however, our report will not _____ this. (imply, infer; lacks, lax)

9. In discussing the change in _____, an _____ scientist will indicate _____ a new Ice Age is _____. (eminent, imminent; weather, whether)

10. Working on _____ parts of the newspaper, two lonely _____ had a _____ _____. (correspondence, correspondents; discrete, discreet)

SEQUENCE U EXERCISES

U•1	dense, dents; grate, great
U•2	canvas, canvass; device, devise
U•3	ate, eight; incredible, incredulous
U•4	clothes, cloths; personal, personnel
U•5	its, it's; affect, effect
U•6	principal, principle; tenant, tenet
U•7	morning, mourning; rain, reign
U•8	abscess, absence; council, counsel
U•9	boy, buoy; coward, cowered
U•10	hour, our; since, sense

U•1

FOCUS   *Dense:* thick; stupid
Dents: hollow places—as from blows

Grate: to grind by scraping; an iron frame for burning fuel
Great: large; distinguished

STUDY   The workman was angered by a supervisor.
The supervisor was unbelievably dense.
The workman pounded dents in a grate.
The dents were great.

WRITE   Angered _____

who _____,

the _____.

CHECK   The workman, angered by

an unbelievably _____

supervisor, pounded _____

_____ in a _____.

U•2

FOCUS   *Canvas:* rough, heavy cloth
Canvass: to solicit

Device: a contrivance
Devise: to make or improvise

STUDY   You devise a plan.
The plan is to canvass voters.
I'll plan a device.
The device will be made of canvas.

WRITE   You _____;

meanwhile, _____.

CHECK   I'll plan a _____

_____ while you _____

a plan to _____ voters.

U•3

FOCUS   *Ate:* consumed
Eight: a number

115

Incredible: too unusual to be possible
Incredulous: unwilling to believe

STUDY Our group was incredulous.
Jumbo ate all the edibles.
He was an incredible eater.
The edibles were in eight dishes.

WRITE Our _____

because _____, _____,

ate _____.

CHECK When Jumbo, an _____

eater, _____ all the edi-

bles in _____ dishes, our

group was _____.

Personal: private, individual
Personnel: persons employed at work

STUDY The personnel changed their clothes.
They grabbed dust cloths.
They made an effort to clean up.
The effort was personal.

WRITE The _____,

grabbed _____,

and _____.

CHECK Changing their _____

and grabbing dust _____,

the _____ made a _____
effort to clean up.

U·4

FOCUS *Clothes:* wearing apparel
Cloths: pieces of woven fabric

U·5

FOCUS *Its:* belonging to it
It's: it is

Affect: to influence (used here as a verb)
Effect: result (used here as a noun)

STUDY It's safe to say something.
The recession did not affect bureaucrats.
Bureaucrats are the umpires in the economic game.
Its effect on small business was devastating.

WRITE _____

_____ bureaucrats,

the _____,

but _____.

CHECK While _____ safe to say that the recession did not

_____ bureaucrats, who umpire the economic game, _____

_____ on small business was devastating.

U•6

FOCUS *Principal:* head of a school; an amount of capital (money)
Principle: fundamental truth, law

Tenant: one who pays rent to occupy a property
Tenet: principle, belief held as truth

STUDY A farmer has his principles.
The farmer is a tenant.
A principal has her tenets.
The tenets are educational.

WRITE A _____

just as _____

_____.

CHECK Like a _____ farmer

who has his _____, a

_____ has her education-

al _____.

U•7

FOCUS *Morning:* early part of the day
Mourning: a state of sorrow, grief

Rain: water falling from clouds
Reign: royal power; to prevail

STUDY Rain marked the end of the king's reign.
The rain was in the early morning.
It marked the beginning of mourning.
The mourning was national.

WRITE Early _____

_____

and _____.

CHECK The end of the king's

_____—and the beginning

of national _____—were

marked by early _____

_____.

U•8

FOCUS *Abscess:* inflamed body tissue
Absence: nonattendance

Council: an administrative body
Counsel: advice; a legal adviser

STUDY   My legal counsel was sent to the meeting.
The meeting was of the city council.
An abscess made my absence excusable.
The abscess was in my wisdom tooth.

WRITE   My _____

_____

even though _____

made _____.

CHECK   An _____ in my wisdom tooth made my _____

from the city _____'s meeting excusable; however, my

legal _____ was sent to it.

U•9

FOCUS   *Boy:* a young male
Buoy: a floating object used as a marker

Coward: one who lacks courage
Cowered: crouched in fear

STUDY   The boy swam to a distant buoy.
The boy had been called a coward.
A crowd called him coward.
The crowd cowered on the shore.

WRITE   _____, who _____

_____

_____, swam _____.

CHECK   After being called a _____

by a crowd that _____

on the shore, the _____

swam to a distant _____.

U•10

FOCUS   *Hour:* sixty minutes
Our: belonging to us

Since: connector meaning "because" or expressing time
Sense: to feel or perceive; something that is reasonable

STUDY   She concluded something last night.
Our proposal made sense.
The proposal was to work by the hour.
We are to be awarded the job.

WRITE   She _____

that _____

_____,

we _____.

CHECK   _____ last night she

concluded that _____ pro-

posal to work by the _____

made _____, we are to be awarded the job.

MASTERY QUIZ U

To demonstrate your mastery of words in Sequence U exercises, write out the following sentences in your own notebook, with the correct words filled in. (Do not check back to the exercises for definitions.)

1. _____ of _____ size were pounded in a _____ by a workman, angered by his unbelievably _____ supervisor. (dense, dents; grate, great)

2. If you'll _____ a plan to _____ voters, I'll plan a _____ _____. (canvas, canvass; device, devise)

3. All the edibles in _____ dishes were eaten by Jumbo, an _____ eater; our group was _____. (ate, eight; incredible, incredulous)

4. Making a _____ effort to clean up, the _____ changed their _____ and grabbed dust _____. (clothes, cloths; personal, personnel)

5. _____ safe to say that the recession had a devastating _____ on small business but that it did not _____ bureaucrats, the umpires in the economic game. (its, it's; affect, effect)

6. Educational _____ are held by a _____; by the same token, a _____ farmer has his _____. (principal, principles; tenant, tenets)

7. The beginning of national _____ —the end of the king's _____— was marked by early _____ _____. (morning, mourning; rain, reign)

8. While my _____ from the city _____ meeting was excusable because of the _____ in my wisdom tooth, my legal _____ was sent to it. (abscess, absence; council, counsel)

9. Called a _____ by a crowd that _____ on the shore, the _____ swam to a distant _____. (boy, buoy; coward, cowered)

10. We are to be awarded the job, _____ she concluded last night that _____ proposal to work by the _____ made _____. (hour, our; since, sense)

SEQUENCE V EXERCISES

V•1   mail, male; cent, scent, sent
V•2   pair, pear; to, too, two
V•3   quiet, quit, quite; personal, personnel
V•4   medal, metal; statue, stature, statute
V•5   prince, prints; praise, prays, preys
V•6   right, rite, write; scene, seen
V•7   allusion, illusion; their, there, they're
V•8   cite, sight, site; miner, minor
V•9   bare, bear; medal, meddle, metal
V•10   passed, past; hearse, hoarse, horse

V•1

FOCUS   *Mail:* letters, packages; flexible armor
Male: of the masculine sex; a man

Cent: a penny, one-hundredth part of a dollar
Scent: a fragrance
Sent: dispatched

STUDY   Any male will like our new scent.
It costs only a few cents per use.
It is sent by mail order only.

WRITE   Any _____,

which _____

and is _____.

CHECK   Our new _____—

which costs only a few _____

per use and is _____ by

_____ order only—will be

liked by any _____.

V•2

FOCUS   *Pair:* two of a kind
Pear: a fruit

To: a preposition meaning "toward"; an infinitive marker
Too: denoting excess
Two: a couple

STUDY   The two soldiers finally decided to pair up.
They had been assigned a patrol.
The patrol was in the pear orchard.
They were not too happy about it.

WRITE   _____ who had _____

_____

120

finally _____;

but _____.

CHECK Although they were not

_____ happy about it, the

_____ soldiers who had

been assigned _____ pa-

trol the _____ orchard fi-

nally decided _____ _____

up.

V•3

FOCUS *Quiet:* silent
    Quit: leave, resign
    Quite: truly, completely, entirely

    Personal: private, individual
    Personnel: persons employed at work

STUDY My feeling is quite strong.
    The feeling is personal.
    The personnel were the quiet ones.
    The personnel decided to quit.

WRITE My _____

that _____

were _____.

CHECK My _____ feeling is

_____ strong: The _____

_____ were the ones who

decided to _____.

V•4

FOCUS *Medal:* an award
    Metal: gold, silver, etc.

Statue: a solid carving or model
Stature: standing, quality
Statute: a law

STUDY The artist was awarded a medal.
    His stature was widely renowned.
    The medal was for his metal statue.
    A pornography statute prohibited its unveiling.

WRITE _____, whose _____

_____, was awarded _____

for _____,

but _____.

CHECK Although the artist's _____
was widely renowned—and although he was awarded a

_____ for his _____

_____—a pornography

_____ prohibited its unveiling.

V•5

FOCUS *Prince:* a king's son
    Prints: images, pictures (noun); publishes (verb)

    Praise: to glorify
    Prays: petitions (God); offers a prayer
    Preys: hunts; victimizes

STUDY A prince preys on the poor.
    A prince prints slogans.
    The slogans praise his own rule.
    Everyone prays for an assassin.

WRITE When _____

and _____,

everyone _____.

CHECK Everyone _____ for an assassin for two reasons: The _____ _____ on the poor and then _____ slogans that _____ his own rule.

V·6

FOCUS *Right:* correct; a legal privilege
Rite: a ceremonial act
Write: to form letters and words

Scene: a sight; part of a play
Seen: observed
STUDY The director had seen a tribal rite.
She felt it was right for filming.
She first had to write for permission.
The permission was to shoot the scene.

WRITE The _____

that _____,

but _____

_____.

CHECK Although she had _____ a tribal _____ that she felt was _____ for filming, the director first had to _____ for permission to shoot the _____.

V·7

FOCUS *Allusion:* an indirect or casual reference
Illusion: a false idea; an unreal appearance

Their: belonging to them
There: in or at that place
They're: they are
STUDY There seems to be agreement.
Their allusion creates an illusion.
Their allusion is to literary works.
The illusion is they've read the books.

WRITE There _____

that _____

creates _____.

CHECK _____ seems to be agreement: by making _____ to literary works, _____ creating the _____ they've read the books.

V·8

FOCUS *Cite:* to quote or mention as an example; to summon before a court
Sight: a vision
Site: a location or scene

Miner: a worker in mines
Minor: one who is underage; a musical term; less important
STUDY The police officer cited a miner.
The citation was for a "minor violation."

Then she sighted her own husband.
Her husband was speeding to a building site.

WRITE The _____

for _____,

and _____,

who _____.

CHECK It was only as the police of-

ficer _____ a _____

for a "_____ violation"

that she _____ her own
husband speeding to a building

_____.

V•9

FOCUS *Bare:* naked
Bear: an animal; to carry

Medal: an award
Meddle: to interfere
Metal: gold, silver, etc.

STUDY Perhaps you shouldn't med-
dle with the metal worker.
The metal worker is built like a bear.
The metal worker has won a medal.
The medal is for fighting bare-fisted.

WRITE Perhaps _____

who _____

and has _____

_____.

CHECK Perhaps you shouldn't

_____ with the _____-

like _____ worker who

has won a _____ for

_____-fisted fighting.

V•10

FOCUS *Passed:* went forward; handed
(here, used with *away* = died)
Past: previous; gone by

Hearse: vehicle used in a funeral
Hoarse: husky, weak-voiced
Horse: an animal

STUDY The trainer watched a hearse.
The hearse drove slowly past.
She thought about her horse.
The horse had just passed away.
She felt her throat get hoarse.

WRITE The _____

_____,

thought _____

_____,

and felt _____.

CHECK Watching a _____ that

drove slowly _____ and

thinking about her _____

that had just _____

away, the trainer felt her throat

get _____.

MASTERY QUIZ V

To demonstrate your mastery of words in Sequence V exercises, write out the following sentences in your own notebook, with the correct words filled in. (Do not check back to the exercises for definitions.)

1. _____ by _____ order only, our new _____, which costs only a few _____ per use, will be liked by any _____. (mail, male; cents, scent, sent)

2. _____ soldiers assigned _____ patrol a _____ orchard finally decided to _____ up; however, they were not _____ happy about it. (pair, pear; to, too, two)

3. I am _____ strong in my _____ feeling that the _____ who decided to _____ were the _____ ones. (quiet, quit, quite; personal, personnel)

4. A pornography _____ prohibited the unveiling of the _____, despite the fact that the artist was awarded a _____ and his _____ was widely renowned. (medal, metal; statue, stature, statute)

5. When a _____ _____ slogans that _____ his own rule and then _____ on the poor, everyone _____ for an assassin. (prince, prints; praise, prays, preys)

6. A tribal _____ that was _____ for filming had been _____ by the director; however, she first had to _____ for permission to shoot the _____. (right, rite, write; scene, seen)

7. By making _____ _____ to literary works, _____ creating the _____ that they've read the books. (allusion, illusion; their, there, they're)

8. As she _____ a _____ for a "_____ violation," the police officer _____ her own husband, who was speeding to a building _____. (cited, sighted, site; miner, minor)

9. To _____ with a _____ worker who is built like a _____ and who has won a _____ for fighting _____-fisted is perhaps something you shouldn't do. (bare, bear; medal, meddle, metal)

10. As the _____ drove slowly _____, the trainer thought about her _____ that had just _____ away and felt her throat get _____. (passed, past; hearse, hoarse, horse)

SEQUENCE W EXERCISES

W•1   heard, herd; roomer, rumors; their, they're
W•2   all together, altogether; hear, here; too, two
W•3   sense, since; your, you're; shore, sure
W•4   son, sun; setting, sitting; raise, rays
W•5   guess, guest; meat, meet; mince, mints
W•6   sighs, size; your, you're; waist, waste
W•7   quiet, quite; tense, tents; too, two
W•8   advice, advise; council, counsel; we'd, weed
W•9   your, you're; shore, sure; loose, lose
W•10   sew, so, sow; their, they're; your, you're

W•1

FOCUS   *Heard:* listened to
     Herd: a large number of animals; to drive or direct a large number of animals

     Roomers: people who rent rooms
     Rumors: talk not based on fact

     Their: belonging to them
     They're: they are

STUDY   I've heard ominous rumors. They're about to herd their roomers out.

WRITE   I've _____

   that _____.

CHECK   According to ominous

     _____ that I've _____,

     _____ about to _____

     _____ _____ out.

126

W•2

FOCUS   *All together:* in one place
     Altogether: completely; on the whole

     Hear: to listen
     Here: in this place

     Too: denoting excess
     Two: a couple

STUDY   The two classes are all together in here.
It's altogether too noisy to hear music.

WRITE   With _____,

   it's _____.

CHECK   It's _____ _____

   noisy to _____ music

   when the _____ classes

   are _____ in _____.

W•3

FOCUS *Sense:* to feel, perceive; something that is reasonable
Since: connector meaning *because* or expressing time

Your: belonging to you
You're: you are

Shore: land at water's edge
Sure: something that will not fail, certain

STUDY Your bags are packed.
I sense something.
You're sure of shore leave.

WRITE _____,

I _____ leave.

CHECK I _____ that _____

_____ bags are packed,

_____ _____ of

_____ leave.

W•4

FOCUS *Son:* a male child
Sun: the star that provides light and heat

Setting: scenery, background
Sitting: resting in an upright position

Raise: to lift; to cause to grow; a salary increase
Rays: beams of light

STUDY The sun's rays were just setting.

The committee was sitting together.
The committee debated my son's raise.

WRITE The _____

as the committee, _____,

debated _____.

CHECK _____ together, the committee debated my

_____'s _____ just as

the _____'s _____

were _____.

W•5

FOCUS *Guess:* to speculate about
Guest: a visitor

Meat: food, flesh of animals
Meet: to come upon, encounter; to come together

Mince: to grind
Mints: candy

STUDY You guess the number of mints.
You meet our guest.
I'll mince the meat.

WRITE If _____

and _____,

I'll _____.

CHECK You _____ the number of _____ and _____

our _____; meanwhile,

I'll _____ the _____.

W•6

FOCUS *Sighs:* long, deep, audible breaths
Size: dimension or magnitude

Your: belonging to you
You're: you are

Waist: part of the body between ribs and hips
Waste: unused

STUDY "Your waist size indicates something."
"You're not letting food go to waste."
She sighs with regret.

WRITE "_____

that _____,"

she _____.

CHECK Regretfully, she _____,

"_____ _____

_____ indicates that

_____ not letting food go

to _____."

W•7

FOCUS *Quiet:* silent
Quite: truly, completely, entirely

Tense: taut; ill-at-ease
Tents: portable canvas shelters

Too: denoting excess
Two: a couple

STUDY The two were quite tense.

They were a little too quiet.
They went to their tents.

WRITE The _____

and _____

as _____.

CHECK _____ _____

and a little _____

_____, the _____

went to their _____.

W•8

FOCUS *Advice:* counsel (noun)
Advise: to give advice to (verb)

Council: an administrative body
Counsel: advice; a legal adviser

We'd: we would
Weed: undesirable, uncultivated plant

STUDY The council's advice was unanimous.
"We'd advise you to take our counsel."
"We'd advise you to mow your weed patch."

WRITE _____:

"_____

and _____."

CHECK "_____ _____

you to take our _____

and mow your _____

patch," was the _____'s

unanimous _____.

W•9

FOCUS *Your:* belonging to you
You're: you are

Shore: land at water's edge
Sure: something that will not fail, certain

Loose: free, escaped; unbound, not tight
Lose: to mislay, become unable to find

STUDY You're sure to lose your change.
The change is loose.
The loss will be on shore leave.

WRITE _____

_____ leave.

CHECK On _____, _____

_____ to _____

_____ _____ change.

W•10

FOCUS *Sew:* to stitch with needle and thread
So: connector meaning "hence," "in order that"
Sow: to scatter seeds

Their: belonging to them
They're: they are

Your: belonging to you
You're: you are

STUDY They're going to sew your clothes.
You're going to sow their seed.
No one has to spend money.

WRITE _____,

and _____;

_____.

CHECK _____ no one has to

spend money, _____ going

to _____ _____ clothes

and _____ going to _____

_____ seed.

MASTERY QUIZ W

To demonstrate your mastery of words in Sequence W exercises, write out the following sentences in your own notebook, with the correct words filled in. (Do not check back to the exercises for definitions.)

1. Ominous _____ that I've _____ indicate that _____ about to _____ _____ _____ out. (heard, herd; roomers, rumors; their, they're)

2. When the _____ classes are _____ in _____, it's _____ _____ noisy to _____ music. (all together, altogether; hear, here; too, two)

3. I _____ that _____ _____ of _____ leave _____ _____ bags are packed. (sense, since; your, you're; shore, sure)

4. With the _____'s _____ just _____, the committee that was _____ together debated my _____'s _____. (son, sun; setting, sitting; raise, rays)

5. I'll _____ the _____ while you _____ the number of _____ and _____ our _____. (guess, guest; meat, meet; mince, mints)

6. "What the _____ of _____ _____ indicates," she _____ with regret, "is that _____ not letting food go to _____." (sighs, size; your, you're; waist, waste)

7. In going to their _____, the _____ were _____ _____ and a little _____ _____. (quiet, quite; tense, tents; too, two)

8. The _____ of the _____—"_____ _____ you to take our _____ and mow your _____ patch"—was unanimous. (advice, advise; council, counsel; we'd, weed)

9. _____ _____ change is _____ to be lost while _____ on _____ leave. (your, you're; shore, sure; loose, lose)

10. _____ going to _____ _____ clothes, and _____ going to _____ _____ seed, _____ no money will be spent. (sew, so, sow; their, they're; your, you're)

SEQUENCE X EXERCISES

X•1 breath, breathe; though, through; weak, week
X•2 their, they're; incest, insist; right, write
X•3 core, corps; fair, fare; some, sum
X•4 paced, paste; pail, pale; serf, surf
X•5 biding, bidding; advice, advise; stake, steak
X•6 accept, except; do, due; passed, past
X•7 imply, infer; your, you're; allusion, illusion
X•8 assistance, assistants; berth, birth; quiet, quite
X•9 board, bored; staid, stayed; were, where
X•10 allowed, aloud; weather, whether; cell, sell

X•1

FOCUS *Breath:* air taken into the lungs and let out
Breathe: to inhale and exhale

Though: in spite of the fact
Through: in one side, out the other; finished; during

Weak: lacking strength
Week: seven days

STUDY She continued to breathe through the week.
This was even though she soon grew weak.
Each breath seemed increasingly labored.

WRITE She _____,

even _____

and _____.

CHECK Even _____ she soon

grew _____ and each

_____ seemed increasingly labored, she continued to

_____ _____ the

_____.

X•2

FOCUS *Their:* belonging to them
They're: they are

Incest: a sexual crime
Insist: to take a stand

Right: a legal privilege; correct, appropriate
Write: to form letters and words

STUDY They're sure to stir controversy.
They insist on something.
It's their right to write.
The writing will be about incest.

131

WRITE _____

because _____

_____.

CHECK Since they _____ on

_____ _____ to _____

about _____, _____

sure to stir controversy.

X•3

FOCUS *Core:* center portion
Corps: people under common direction

Fair: beautiful; just, right; a carnival, exhibition
Fare: price charged for transporting a passenger

Some: an unspecified quantity
Sum: total; an amount of money

STUDY Some "hard core" marines stayed in camp.
Others of the corps paid a handsome sum.
The sum was for train fare.
The train fare was to the fair.

WRITE _____;

however, _____

for _____.

CHECK Although _____ "hard

_____" marines stayed in

camp, others of the _____

paid a handsome _____

for train _____ to the

_____.

X•4

FOCUS *Paced:* strode up and down
Paste: glue; a moist, smooth preparation

Pail: a bucket
Pale: whitish colored

Serf: a slave
Surf: the waves of the sea

STUDY: The serf paced near the surf.
The serf mixed a paste.
The paste was pale yellow.
The paste was in a pail.

WRITE Before mixing _____

_____,

the _____.

CHECK As he _____ near the

_____, the _____

mixed a _____ yellow

_____ in a _____.

X•5

FOCUS *Biding:* staying, waiting
Bidding: offering of money

Advice: counsel (noun)
Advise: to give advice to (verb)

Stake: a wager; piece of wood; at risk
Steak: meat

STUDY We'd advise biding your time.
This is in bidding.
A steak dinner is at stake.

This comes from taking our advice.

WRITE We'd _____

because _____

_____

from _____.

CHECK Because a _____ din-

ner is at _____ from tak-

ing our _____, we'd

_____ _____ your

time in the _____.

X•6

FOCUS *Accept:* to receive; to approve
Except: to leave out or take out

Do: to perform
Due: owed

Passed: went forward; handed
Past: previous; gone by
STUDY We do not accept assignments.
The assignments are past due.
There is an exception.
We are passed a modest bribe.

WRITE We _____

that _____,

_____.

CHECK Assignments that are _____

_____ we do not _____

—_____ when we are

_____ a modest bribe.

X•7

FOCUS *Imply:* to hint, suggest
Infer: to conclude by reasoning

Your: belonging to you
You're: you are

Allusion: indirect or casual reference
Illusion: false idea; unreal appearance
STUDY I infer something from your allusion.
Your allusion is to the word *fake*.
You're going to imply something.
My sincerity is an illusion.

WRITE I _____

that _____.

CHECK From _____ _____

to the word *fake*, I _____

that _____ going to _____

my sincerity is an _____.

X•8

FOCUS *Assistance:* help, aid
Assistants: helpers, aides

Berth: built-in bed
Birth: the act of being born

Quiet: silent
Quite: truly, completely, entirely
STUDY The berth was quite crowded.
The berth was surprisingly quiet.
Assistants provided assistance.
The woman easily gave birth.

WRITE The _____

_____

as _____,

and _____.

CHECK _____ provided _____
to a woman who easily gave

_____ in a _____

that was _____ crowded

yet surprisingly _____.

X•9

FOCUS *Board:* timber, piece of
wood; group of people
Bored: wearied by dullness;
pierced

Staid: sober, solemn, quiet
Stayed: remained

Were: past tense of *be*
Where: in or at what place

STUDY We were totally bored.
We stayed through the meeting.
Board members debated policy
there.
They were staid.

WRITE Although _____,

we _____

_____.

CHECK We _____ totally _____;

nevertheless, we _____

through the meeting _____

_____ _____ mem-
bers debated policy.

X•10

FOCUS *Allowed:* permitted
Aloud: not silently

Weather: condition of the atmosphere
Whether: if (used here as a connector)

Cell: a small prison room
Sell: to exchange for money
STUDY   The thief paced his cell.
He talked aloud about the weather.
He also asked something.
Would he be allowed to sell stolen goods?

WRITE   The _____,

talked _____,

and _____

_____.

CHECK   Talking _____ about

the _____ and asking

_____ he'd be _____

to _____ stolen goods,

the thief paced his _____.

MASTERY QUIZ X

To demonstrate your mastery of words in Sequence X exercises, write out the following sentences in your own notebook, with the correct words filled in. (Do not check back to the exercises for definitions.)

1. She soon grew _____, even _____ she continued to _____ _____ the _____, with each _____ increasingly labored. (breath, breathe; though, through; weak, week)

2. _____ sure to stir controversy; they _____ on _____ _____ to _____ about _____. (their, they're; incest, insist; right, write)

3. _____ of the marine _____ paid a handsome _____ for train _____ to the _____, but the "hard _____" of them stayed in camp. (core, corps; fair, fare; some, sum)

4. The _____, mixing a _____ yellow _____ in a _____, _____ near the _____. (paced, paste; pail, pale; serf, surf)

MASTERY QUIZ X
CONTINUED

5. At _____ for taking our _____ is a _____ dinner; so we'd _____ _____ your time in the _____. (biding, bidding; advice, advise; stake, steak)

6. _____ when we are _____ a modest bribe, we _____ not _____ assignments that are _____ _____. (accept, except; do, due; passed, past)

7. What I _____ from _____ _____ to the word *fake* is that _____ going to _____ my sincerity is an _____. (imply, infer; your, you're; allusion, illusion)

8. The _____ where _____ provided _____ to a woman who easily gave _____ was _____ crowded but surprisingly _____. (assistance, assistants; berth, birth; quiet, quite)

9. As we _____ through the meeting _____ _____ _____ members debated policy, we _____ totally _____. (board, bored; staid, stayed; were, where)

10. Pacing his _____ and talking _____ about the _____, the thief asked _____ he'd be _____ to _____ stolen goods. (allowed, aloud; weather, whether; cell, sell)

SEQUENCE Y EXERCISES

Y·1   complements, compliments; its, it's; right, write
Y·2   brake, break; hour, our; wear, where
Y·3   knew, new; went, when; thorough, through
Y·4   sat, set; laying, lying; tracked, tract
Y·5   desert, dessert; read, red; passed, past
Y·6   plane, plain; stair, stare; wood, would
Y·7   chance, chants; lead, led; hoard, horde
Y·8   confidant, confident; know, no; one, won
Y·9   local, locale; muscles, mussels; pedal, peddle
Y·10   all ready, already; lessen, lesson; right, write

Y·1

FOCUS   *Complements:* completes, makes perfect
Compliments: expressions of praise

Its: belonging to it
It's: it is

Right: a legal privilege, correct; appropriate
Write: to form letters and words

STUDY   It's my intent to write something.
This wine is bound to win compliments.
Its taste complements macaroni and cheese.
Its taste is especially right with liver.

WRITE _____

that _____

because _____

and _____.

CHECK   Because _____ taste

not only _____ macaroni and cheese but is especially

_____ with liver, _____

my intent to _____
that this wine is sure to win

_____.

Y·2

FOCUS   *Brake:* device used to stop a vehicle
Break: to smash; an interval, gap, or rest

Hour: sixty minutes
Our: belonging to us

137

Wear: to carry on one's body; to weaken, harass
Where: in or at what place

STUDY We wondered during our break.
The break lasted an hour.
Where had the linings started to wear?
The linings were for the brakes.

WRITE We _____,

which _____,

_____.

CHECK It was during _____

_____, which lasted an

_____, that we wondered

_____ the _____ lin-

ings had started to _____.

Y•3

FOCUS *Knew:* perceived or under-stood
New: fresh or unused

Went: past tense of *go*
When: connector meaning "at the time"

Thorough: diligent, complete
Through: in one side, out the other; finished

STUDY John went through the new house.
He made a search for locks.
The search was very thorough.
We knew something was unusual.

WRITE _____

and _____,

we _____.

CHECK We _____ something

was unusual _____ John

_____ _____ the

_____ house and made a

_____ search for locks.

Y•4

FOCUS *Sat:* past tense of *sit*
Set: to place something; to adjust

Laying: devising, making, set-ting forth
Lying: reclining; telling a false-hood

Tracked: followed; traced
Tract: an expanse of land; a pamphlet

STUDY I sat down to set my compass.
I tracked footprints across the tract.
I found a man lying in the snow.
He was laying plans to ambush me.

WRITE I _____,

_____,

and _____

who _____.

CHECK To _____ my com-

pass, I _____ down; then,

after I _____ footprints

across the _____, I found

SEQUENCE Y EXERCISES **139**

a man _____ in the snow
who was _____ plans to
ambush me.

Y·5

FOCUS *Desert:* to abandon; a dry
piece of land
Dessert: last course of a meal

Read: looked at; perused
Red: a color

Passed: went forward; handed
Past: previous; gone by
STUDY She had read something in
past accounts.
Folks passed through the desert.
The desert was red.
They desperately wanted dessert.

WRITE She _____

that _____

because _____.

CHECK According to _____ ac-

counts that she had _____,

folks _____ through the

_____ _____ be-

cause they desperately wanted

_____.

Y·6

FOCUS *Plane:* aircraft; a tool for
woodworking; flat, level surface
Plain: clear; simple, unadorned

Stair: one of a flight of steps
Stare: gaze (used here as a verb)

Wood: a thick collection of trees;
lumber, timber
Would: will
STUDY I love to work with wood.
I'd first stare at the stair.
The stair was very plain.
Then I would carefully plane its
railing.

WRITE Since _____,

I'd _____,

and _____.

CHECK I love to work with _____;

therefore, I'd first _____ at

the very _____ _____,

and then I _____ careful-

ly _____ its railing.

Y·7

FOCUS *Chance:* accidentally,
without plan
Chants: melodies, songs

Lead: a metal
Led: guided

Hoard: a hidden supply
Horde: a crowd, swarm
STUDY A native horde made chants.
The chants led us to a hoard.
The leading was only by chance.
The hoard was of lead weights.

WRITE A _____

that _____

to _____.

CHECK   It was only by _____

that _____ from a native

_____ _____ us to

a _____ of _____

weights.

Y•8

FOCUS   *Confidant:* a close, trusted friend
Confident: certain, sure of oneself

Know: to be well-informed about
No: deny, refuse

One: single unit; a certain person
Won: finished first; succeeded; gained

STUDY   I had won the jackpot.
I was naively confident.
My confidant would know enough.
My confidant would tell no one.

WRITE   I _____;

however, _____

that _____

to _____.

CHECK   After I had _____ the

jackpot, I was naively _____

that my _____ would

_____ enough to tell _____

_____.

Y•9

FOCUS   *Local:* related to a small area
Locale: location, area

Muscles: fibrous tissues that produce movement
Mussels: mollusks

Pedal: to work the pedals—e.g., of a bike (used here as a verb)
Peddle: to go from place to place selling

STUDY   Nick wanted to build up his leg muscles.
He agreed to pedal all over the locale.
He would try to peddle mussels.
The mussels were local.

WRITE   Because he _____,

Nick _____,

trying _____.

CHECK   Intent on building up his

leg _____, Nick agreed

to _____ all over the

_____ in an effort to

_____ _____ _____.

Y•10

FOCUS   *All ready:* prepared
Already: by or before given time

Lessen: to diminish
Lesson: an assignment to be studied

Right: a legal privilege; correct, appropriate
Write: to form letters and words
STUDY   The lesson has already been discussed.
We're all ready to write.
Someone asks about the right approach.
This only lessens our writing time.
WRITE   The _____,

and _____

when _____,
which _____.
CHECK When the _____ has

_____ been discussed and

we're _____ to _____,

someone asks about the _____

approach, which only _____
our time for writing.

MASTERY QUIZ Y

To demonstrate your mastery of words in Sequence Y exercises, write out the following sentences in your own notebook, with the correct words filled in. (Do not check back to the exercises for definitions.)

1. _____ my intent to _____ that this wine is bound to win

   _____; _____ taste not only _____ macaroni and

   cheese but is especially _____ with liver. (complements, compliments; its, it's; right, write)

2. _____ _____ lasted an _____; during it, we wondered _____ the _____ linings had started to _____. (brake, break; hour, our; wear, where)

3. It was _____ John _____ _____ the _____

   house and made a very _____ search for locks that we

   _____ something was unusual. (knew, new; went, when; thorough, through)

4. I _____ down to _____ my compass; then, after I had

   _____ footprints across the _____, I found a man _____

   in the snow who was _____ plans to ambush me. (sat, set; laying, lying; tracked, tract)

MASTERY QUIZ Y
CONTINUED

5. In _____ accounts that she had _____, folks _____ through the _____ _____ because they desperately wanted _____. (desert, dessert; read, red; passed, past)

6. My love for working with _____ is such that I'd first _____ at the very _____ _____, and then I _____ carefully _____ its railing. (plain, plane; stair, stare; wood, would)

7. Only by _____ were we _____ to a _____ of _____ weights as the native _____ made _____. (chance, chants; lead, led; hoard, horde)

8. What I had _____ was the jackpot; but I was naively _____: My _____ would _____ enough to tell _____ _____. (confidant, confident; know, no; one, won)

9. Nick wanted to build up his leg _____; consequently, he agreed to _____ all over the _____ and try to _____ _____ that were _____. (local, locale; muscles, mussels; pedal, peddle)

10. The _____ has _____ been discussed and we're _____ to _____; then someone asks about the _____ approach and only _____ our writing time. (all ready, already; lessens, lesson; right, write)

SEQUENCE Z EXERCISES

Z•1   its, it's; thorough, through; elicit, illicit
Z•2   rite, write; role, roll; idle, idol
Z•3   choose, chose; their, there, they're; root, route
Z•4   read, red; suit, suite, sweet; wear, where
Z•5   potent, potion; vial, vile; which, witch
Z•6   knew, new; loose, lose; real, reel
Z•7   advice, advise; complements, compliments; ingenious, ingenuous
Z•8   lessen, lesson; moral, morale; depravity, deprivation
Z•9   dew, due; setting, settling, sitting; some, sum
Z•10 diner, dinner; to, too, two; hour, our; buy, by

Z•1

FOCUS   *Its:* belonging to it
It's: it is

Thorough: diligent, complete
Through: in one side, out the other; finished; during

Elicit: to draw forth, evoke
Illicit: unlawful

STUDY   Something happens through questioning.
The questioning is very thorough.
The agency manages to elicit its confessions.
The confessions concern illicit drug sales.

WRITE _____

_____

that _____

concerning _____.

CHECK   The   agency   manages,

_____ very _____

questioning, to _____ _____

confessions about _____
drug sales.

Z•2

FOCUS   *Rite:* a ceremonial act
Write: to form words on paper

Role: actor's part
Roll: to move; a list of names

Idle: useless, not busy, lazy
Idol: image, object of worship

STUDY   Calling the roll was a rite.
The rite happened daily.
Our role was to remain idle.
Our idol would write down absentees.

143

WRITE Calling _____

during which _____

while _____

CHECK During the _____ call,

a daily _____, it was our

_____ to remain _____

while our _____ would

_____ down absentees.

Z•3

FOCUS *Choose:* to select or decide
Chose: past tense of *choose*

Their: belonging to them
There: in or at that place
They're: they are

Root: part of a plant; the source, essential part
Route: road pathway

STUDY The root of their problem is simple.
They're in a hurry to get there.
They're going to choose a route.
No one else chose it.

WRITE The _____:

_____,

and _____

that _____.

CHECK The simple _____ of the problem is that because

_____ in a hurry to get

_____, _____ going to

_____ a _____ that

no one else _____.

Z•4

FOCUS *Read:* looked at; perused
Red: a color

Suit: a set of clothing
Suite: a hotel room
Sweet: luscious, fragrant, pleasing

Wear: to carry on one's body; to weaken, harass
Where: in or at what place

STUDY I've read about the suite.
It was furnished in red.
It was located above a sweet shop.
George elected to wear his "birthday suit" there.

WRITE I've _____—

furnished _____

and _____—

_____.

CHECK The _____ I've _____

about—_____ George e-

lected to _____ his "birth-

day _____"—was furnish-

ed in _____ and located

above a _____ shop.

Z•5

FOCUS *Potent:* having power, effective
Potion: a drink of magic substance

Vial(s): small bottle(s) for liquids
Vile: repulsive, disgusting

Which: what one of several
Witch: a practicer of magic; an old, ugly woman

STUDY   The witch made noises.
The noises were vile.
The witch sipped from two vials.
One vial contained a potion.
The potion was potent.

WRITE   The _____

and _____,

one of _____.

CHECK   _____ noises   were

made   by   a   _____   as she

sipped   from   two   _____,

one   of   _____   contained   a

_____   _____.

Z•6

FOCUS   *Knew:* perceived or under-
stood
New: fresh or unused

Loose: free, escaped; unbound, not tight
Lose: to mislay, become unable to find

Real: actual, true
Reel: spool with wound line

STUDY   All of us knew something.
The reel was very loose.
The reel was new.
We might lose a trophy fish.
The trophy fish was real.

WRITE   _____ that because

_____,

we might _____.

CHECK   Because the _____

_____ was very _____,

all of us _____ that we

might _____ a _____

trophy fish.

Z•7

FOCUS   *Advice:* counsel (noun)
Advise: to give advice to (verb)

Complements: completes, makes perfect
Compliments: expressions of praise

Ingenious: clever, resourceful
Ingenuous: frank, open; artless, naive

STUDY   The consultant's advice was ingenuous.
Advise employees of the company's goals.
Give compliments for marketing.
The marketing is ingenious.
Complement their work with play.

WRITE   The _____:

_____,

give _____,

and _____.

CHECK   The consultant's _____

_____ was to _____

employees of the company's

goals, give _____ for

_____ marketing, and

_____ their work with

play.

Z•8

FOCUS   *Lessen:* to diminish
Lesson: an assignment to be studied

Moral: message; ethical, honorable, good
Morale: mental condition

Depravity: morally bad, corrupt
Deprivation: to keep from having

STUDY   The moral of the lesson is clear.
We lessen deprivation.
We may reduce depravity.
The depravity is moral.
We may improve morale.

WRITE   The _____:

if _____,

we _____

and _____.

CHECK   The clear _____ to

this _____ is that if we

_____ _____, we may

reduce _____

and improve _____.

Z•9

FOCUS   *Dew:* water drops
Due: owed

Setting: scenery, background
Settling: calming, reassuring
Sitting: resting in an upright position

Some: an unspecified quantity
Sum: total; an amount of money

STUDY A huge sum was coming
due.
Dew was settling around them.
They were sitting in a setting.
The setting was beautiful.
They wondered how to raise
money.

WRITE With _____

and _____,

they _____,

wondering _____.

CHECK As they were _____ in

a beautiful _____, won-

dering how to raise _____

money for a huge _____

that was coming _____,

_____ was _____ a-
round them.

Z·10

FOCUS *Diner:* a roadside restaurant
Dinner: a main meal

To: a preposition meaning "toward"; an infinitive marker

Too: denoting excess
Two: a couple

Hour: sixty minutes
Our: belonging to us

Buy: to purchase
By: a preposition meaning
"near," "past"

STUDY Our plan was to drive by
the diner.
Our plan was to buy two burgers.
The burgers would be for dinner.
Our plan was to get back in an
hour.
We were too tired to go out.

WRITE _____,

_____,

and _____;

but _____.

CHECK Although _____ plan

was to drive _____ the

_____, _____ _____

burgers for _____, and

get back in an _____,

we were _____ tired to go
out.

MASTERY QUIZ Z

To demonstrate your mastery of words in Sequence Z exercises, write out the following sentences in your own notebook, with the correct words filled in. (Do not check back to the exercises for definitions.)

1. _____ very _____ questioning, the agency manages to _____ _____ confessions concerning _____ drug sales. (its, it's; thorough, through; elicit, illicit)

2. _____ call was a daily _____; our _____ was to remain _____ while our _____ would _____ down absentees. (rite, write; role, roll; idle, idol)

3. _____ in a hurry to get _____, and _____ going to _____ a _____ no one else _____; that's the simple _____ of _____ problem. (choose, chose; their, there, they're; root, route)

4. Located above a _____ shop was a _____ _____ that I've _____ about; this was _____ George elected to _____ his "birthday _____." (read, red; suit, suite, sweet; wear, where)

5. Sipping from two _____—one of _____ contained a _____ _____—the _____ made _____ noises. (potent, potion; vial(s), vile; which, witch)

6. With the _____ _____ very _____, we all _____ that we might _____ a _____ trophy fish. (knew, new; loose, lose; real, reel)

7. To _____ employees of the company's goals, to give _____ for marketing which was _____, to _____ their work with play—this was the consultant's _____ _____. (advice, advise; complements, compliments; ingenious, ingenuous)

8. Clearly, the _____ of the _____ is that we may reduce _____ _____ and improve _____ if we _____ _____. (lessen, lesson; moral, morale; depravity, deprivation)

MASTERY QUIZ Z
CONTINUED

9. A huge _____ was coming _____, and _____ was _____ around them as they were _____ in a beautiful _____, wondering how to raise _____ money. (dew, due; setting, settling, sitting; some, sum)

10. It was _____ plan, after driving _____ the _____, to _____ _____ burgers for _____ and to get back in an _____; however, we were _____ tired to go. (diner, dinner; to, too, two; hour, our; buy, by)

INDEX

This index lists the location of all exercises dealing with easily confused words (basic vocabulary) in this book.

To use the index, first identify the words you're interested in mastering through sentence combining practice—for example, *its* and *it's*. Then note the location of exercises (letter plus number) for this pair of words (fourteen separate exercises in this instance). Finally, work through these exercises, checking yourself on the Mastery Quiz items as appropriate.

Please note that for the most part this is a double-entry index. That is, you will find words such as *affect* and *effect* under both *A* and *E*. However, certain pairs of words—those that would appear next to each other in the list (such as *angel* and *angle*)—have have been listed only once.

There are over 260 groups of easily confused words in this index.

abscess, absence U-8
accept, except G-8, J-4, Q-6, X-6
access, excess A-8, H-9
acts, ax(e) S-7
advice, advise G-8, R-10, W-8, X-5, Z-7
affect, effect A-10, B-7, C-9, N-9, Q-8,
   R-10, U-5
aid, aide P-4
air, heir M-1, S-4
aisle, I'll L-1
aisle, isle Q-2

all, awl I-1
alley, ally S-10
allot, a lot D-2
allowed, aloud F-6, G-9, T-1, X-10
all ready, already F-3, P-7, Y-10
all together, altogether W-2
allusion, illusion V-7, X-7
ally, alley S-10
aloud, allowed F-6, G-9, T-1, X-10
already, all ready F-3, P-7, Y-10
altar, alter O-10, T-1

altogether, all together   W-2
angel, angle   F-10
ant, aunt   E-3
are, our   P-5
a rest, arrest   E-4
ascent, assent   R-7, S-4
ask, ax(e)   E-1, H-7
assent, ascent   R-7, S-4
assistance, assistants   J-8, X-8
ate, eight   N-7, U-3
aunt, ant   E-3
awl, all   I-1
ax(e), acts   S-7
ax(e), ask   E-1, H-7

bail, bale   T-3
bald, bawled   H-8
bale, bail   T-3
bare, bear   E-9, O-7, V-9
baron, barren   H-8
base, bass   O-6
bawled, bald   H-8
beach, beech   T-2
bear, bare   E-9, O-7, V-9
beat, beet   M-8, T-6
beech, beach   T-2
been, bin   M-2
beet, beat   M-8, T-6
berth, birth   X-8
biding, bidding   N-6, X-5
bin, been   M-2
birth, berth   X-8
blew, blue   H-6
board, bored   J-10, X-9
boarder, border   L-9
bored, board   J-10, X-9
boy, buoy   U-9
brake, break   Y-2
breadth, breath, breathe   D-10, X-1
break, brake   Y-2
breath, breathe, breadth   D-10, X-1
brews, bruise   T-6
bridal, bridle   Q-2
bruise, brews   T-6
buoy, boy   U-9
buy, by   Z-10

canvas, canvass   U-2
capital, capitol   O-9
caught, cot   Q-9
cause, caws   G-3

ceiling, sealing   L-8
cell, sell   X-10
cellar, seller   K-2, N-4
censor, censure   R-6
cent, scent, sent   G-4, V-1
cents, sense   I-6
cereal, serial   P-10
certain, curtain   H-5
chance, chants   I-7, Y-7
chased, chaste   L-3
chef, chief   F-4
chews, choose   I-3
chief, chef   F-4
choose, chews   I-3
choose, chose   L-5, Z-3
cite, sight, site   J-6, R-9, V-8
climb, clime   R-7
close, clothes   S-6
clothes, cloths   U-4
coarse, course   E-2, L-9
colonel, kernel   Q-9
complement, compliment   Y-1, Z-7
confidant, confident   Y-8
core, corps   X-3
correspondence, correspondents   P-10,
   T-10
cot, caught   Q-9
council, counsel   U-8, W-8
course, coarse   E-2, L-9
coward, cowered   U-9
creak, creek   T-2
crews, cruise   A-9, I-3
currant, current   T-5
curtain, certain   H-5

dairy, diary   Q-10
days, daze   Q-3
decent, descent, dissent   D-8, R-6
dense, dents   U-1
depravity, deprivation   Z-8
descent, dissent, decent   D-8, R-6
desert, dessert   M-9, Y-5
device, devise   U-2
dew, do, due   J-2, X-6, Z-9
diary, dairy   Q-10
diner, dinner   M-9, Z-10
discreet, discrete   T-10
discussed, disgust   B-5
dissent, descent, decent   D-8, R-6
do, due, dew   J-2, X-6, Z-9
dual, duel   B-6
due, do, dew   J-2, X-6, Z-9
duel, dual   B-6

effect, affect   A-10, B-7, C-9, N-9, Q-8,
  R-10, U-5
eight, ate   N-7, U-3
elicit, illicit   P-5, Z-1
emigrate, immigrate   S-10
eminent, imminent   T-9
except, accept   G-8, J-4, Z-6, X-6
excess, access   A-8, H-9

faint, feint   L-4
fair, fare   E-6, X-3
feint, faint   L-4
find, fined   O-1
fir, fur   R-2
flaunt, flout   N-10
flour, flower   A-4, M-2
flout, flaunt   N-10
flower, flour   A-4, M-2
foreword, forward   T-5
formal, former   S-6, T-7
formally, formerly   F-9, P-4
forth, fourth   I-5, M-6
fur, fir   R-2

gilt, guilt   P-2
girl, grill   E-10
gorilla, guerrilla   M-10
grate, great   U-1
grill, girl   E-10
grisly, grizzly   G-3, R-2
groan, grown   G-5
grocer, grosser   G-5
grown, groan   G-5
guerrilla, gorilla   M-10
guess, guest   J-5, L-7, Q-6, W-5
guilt, gilt   P-2
gym, Jim   G-2

hair, hare, here   F-3, M-4
hairy, Harry   L-7
hare, hair   M-4
hare, here   F-3
Harry, hairy   L-7
hear, here   E-5, F-1, H-10, J-5, L-5,
  P-1, W-2
heard, herd   M-6, W-1
heard, horde   Y-7
hearse, hoarse, horse   V-10
heir, air   M-1, S-4
he'll, hill   E-3
herd, heard   M-6, W-1
here, hair   F-3

here, hare   M-4
here, hear   E-5, F-1, H-10, J-5, L-5,
  P-1, W-2
higher, hire   P-3
hill, he'll   E-3
him, hymn   E-5, I-7, P-3
hire, higher   P-3
hoarse, horse, hearse   V-10
hole, whole   J-10
holy, wholly   O-9
horde, heard   Y-7
horse, hoarse, hearse   V-10
hour, our   I-4, U-10, Y-2, Z-10
human, humane   M-10
hymn, him   E-5, I-7, P-3

idle, idol   Z-2
I'll, aisle   L-1
I'll, isle   P-1
illicit, elicit   P-5, Z-1
illusion, allusion   V-7, X-7
immigrate, emigrate   S-10
imminent, eminent   T-9
imply, infer   T-8, X-7
incest, insist   X-2
incredible, incredulous   U-3
infer, imply   T-8, X-7
ingenious, ingenuous   Z-7
insist, incest   X-2
isle, aisle   Q-2
isle, I'll   P-1
its, it's   A-6, C-6, D-1, E-6, G-6, H-5,
  I-5, J-1, L-10, M-3, R-3, U-5,
  Y-1, Z-1

Jim, gym   G-2

kernel, colonel   Q-9
knead, need   B-4, K-4
knew, new   E-8, H-3, J-8, R-3, Y-3, Z-6
knight, night   L-3, P-2, R-4
knot, not   E-8, P-8
know, no   Y-8
knows, nose   H-3

lacks, lax   C-7, T-8
laid, lain   P-9
later, latter   T-7
lax, lacks   C-7, T-8
lay, lie   P-9
laying, lying   Y-4
lead, led   M-5, N-8, Y-7
leans, liens   P-6

leased, least N-2
led, lead M-5, N-8, Y-7
lessen, lesson A-5, N-3, Y-10, Z-8
liar, lyre O-6
lie, lay P-9
liens, leans P-6
loan, lone K-4, N-2, P-6
local, locale M-3, Y-9
lone, loan K-4, N-2, P-6
loose, lose A-2, C-8, K-1, W-9, Z-6
lying, laying Y-4
lyre, liar O-6

made, maid E-4, I-9, M-1
mail, male F-9, N-5, R-1, V-1
marshal, martial T-3
meat, meet M-8, O-2, Q-3, W-5
medal, meddle, metal V-4, V-9
meet, meat M-8, O-2, Q-3, W-5
metal, meddle, medal V-4, V-9
mince, mints W-5
mind, mine D-3, K-5, N-8
miner, minor F-6, Q-8, V-8
mints, mince W-5
moral, morale S-9, Z-8
morning, mourning U-7
muscles, mussels Y-9

need, knead B-4, K-4
new, knew E-8, H-3, J-8, R-3, Y-3, Z-6
night, knight L-3, P-2, R-4
no, know Y-8
none, nun F-2, K-7
nose, knows H-3
not, knot E-8, P-8
nun, none F-2, K-7

one, won E-10, F-7, J-4, L-2, O-3, P-8, Y-8
our, are P-5
our, hour I-4, U-10, Y-2, Z-10

paced, paste X-4
pail, pale X-4
pain, pane J-9
pair, pear O-4, V-2
pale, pail X-4
pane, pain J-9
parish, perish S-8
passed, past V-10, X-6, Y-5

paste, paced X-4
patience, patients F-2, K-3
pause, paws O-7
peace, piece K-5, Q-5, T-4
peak, peek Q-5
peal, peel H-10
pear, pair O-4, V-2
pedal, peddle Y-9
peek, peak Q-5
peel, peal H-10
peer, pier N-6
perish, parish S-8
personal, personnel S-9, U-4, V-3
picture, pitcher R-8
piece, peace K-5, Q-5, T-4
pier, peer N-6
pitcher, picture R-8
plain, plane F-8, G-6, K-8, Y-6
pleas, please G-10, K-8, N-4
potent, potion Z-5
praise, pray, prey A-7, T-4, V-5
precede, proceed G-7, J-3
premise, promise J-7
presence, presents F-5, I-4, O-10
pretest, protest G-7
prey, pray, praise A-7, T-4, V-5
pries, prize K-7
prince, prints N-10, O-8, V-5
principal, principle U-6
prints, prince N-10, O-8, V-5
prize, pries K-7
proceed, precede G-7, J-3
profit, prophet B-3, K-6
promise, premise J-7
prophet, profit B-3, K-6
protest, pretest G-7

quiet, quite, quit B-10, E-9, G-1, N-1, V-3, W-7, X-8

rain, reign U-7
raise, rays W-4
read, red F-7, H-7, Y-5, Z-4
real, reel Z-6
red, read F-7, H-7, Y-5, Z-4
reign, rain U-7
residence, residents S-3
retch, wretch M-7
riding, writing Q-10, S-5
right, rite, write V-6, X-2, Y-1, Y-10, Z-2
road, rode I-8

role, roll   Z-2
roomers, rumors   H-4, W-1
root, route   R-4, Z-3
rote, wrote   I-8
route, root   R-4, Z-3
rumors, roomers   H-4, W-1
rye, wry   M-7

sail, sale   I-10, R-1
sat, set   Y-4
scene, seam, seem   B-9
scene, seen   E-7, G-1, L-4, O-4, V-6
scent, sent, cent   G-4, V-1
sea, see   H-6, J-2
sealing, ceiling   L-8
see, sea   H-6, J-2
seem, seam, scene   B-9
seen, scene   E-7, G-1, L-4, O-4, V-6
sell, cell   X-10
seller, cellar   K-2, N-4
sense, cents   I-6
sense, since   J-3, K-9, L-10, N-1, U-10, W-3
sent, scent, cent   G-4, V-1
serf, surf   X-4
serial, cereal   P-10
set, sat   Y-4
setting, settling, sitting   D-9, W-4, Z-9
sew, so, sow   W-10
shore, sure   W-3, W-9
sighs, size   Q-1, W-6
sight, site, cite   J-6, R-9, V-8
since, sense   J-3, K-9, L-10, N-1, U-10
site, sight, cite   J-6, R-9, V-8
sitting, setting, settling   D-9, W-4, Z-9
size, sighs   Q-1, W-6
so, sew, sow   W-10
sole, soul   N-7, R-5
some, sum   X-3, Z-9
son, sun   O-3, Q-7, W-4
soul, sole   N-7, R-5
sow, so, sew   W-10
staid, stayed   L-8, S-3, X-9
stair, stare   L-1, S-1, Y-6
stake, steak   F-4, X-5
stare, stair   L-1, S-1, Y-6
stationary, stationery   S-5
statue, stature, statute   F-10, V-4
stayed, staid   L-8, S-3, X-9
steak, stake   F-4, X-5
steal, steel   M-5
suit, suite, sweet   C-2, S-1, Z-4
sum, some   X-3, Z-9

sun, son   O-3, Q-7, W-4
super, supper   K-6
sure, shore   W-3, W-9
surf, serf   X-4
sweet, suit, suite   C-2, S-1, Z-4

tacks, tax   I-6
tail, tale   M-4
taught, taut   I-10, N-3
tax, tacks   I-6
teas, tease   G-4
tenant, tenet   U-6
tense, tents   Q-4, W-7
than, then   B-2, N-9
there, their, they're   D-5, E-1, F-1, G-9, G-10, H-2, J-1, O-1, R-9, V-7, W-10, X-2, Z-3
thorough, though, threw, through   C-4, Q-7, X-1, Y-3, Z-1
throne, thrown   O-8
through, threw, thorough, though   C-4, Q-7, X-1, Y-3, Z-1
thrown, throne   O-8
tide, tied   S-2
to, too, two   D-6, V-2, W-2, W-7, Z-10
tracked, tract   Y-4
two, too, to   D-6, V-2, W-2, W-7, Z-10

vain, vein   A-3
vain, vane   K-10
vein, vane   K-10
vial, vile   Z-5
vice, vise   S-7
vile, vial   Z-5
vise, vice   S-7

wade, weighed   B-1
waist, waste   W-6
wait, weight   Q-1, S-2
wander, wonder   G-2, H-1
ware, wear   K-2
waste, waist   W-6
way, weigh   K-9
weak, week   Q-4, R-5, S-8, X-1
wear, ware   K-2
wear, where, we're, were   B-8, C-3, I-2, H-1, J-6, L-6, O-5, X-9, Y-2, Z-4
weather, whether   H-2, K-10, T-9, X-10
we'd, weed   W-8
week, weak   Q-4, R-5, S-8, X-1
weigh, way   K-9
weighed, wade   B-1

weight, wait Q-1, S-2
well, we'll, will D-**7**, R-8
went, when Y-3
were, we're, where, wear B-8, C-3, H-1,
    I-2, J-6, L-6, O-5, X-9, Y-2, Z-4
when, went Y-3
when, win H-9
where, were, we're, wear B-8, C-3, H-1,
    I-2, J-6, L-6, O-5, X-9, Y-2, Z-4
whether, weather H-2, K-10, T-9, X-10
which, witch E-7, O-5, P-7, Z-5
whine, wine, win C-1, I-9
whole, hole J-10
wholly, holy O-9
who's, whose C-10, D-4, J-9, N-5
will, well, we'll D-7, R-8

win, when H-9
win, wine, whine C-1, I-9
witch, which E-7, O-5, P-7, Z-5
won, one E-10, F-7, J-4, L-2, O-3, P-8,
    Y-8
wonder, wander G-2, H-1
wood, would F-8, Y-6
wretch, retch M-7
write, rite, right V-6, X-2, Y-1, Y-10, Z-2
writing, riding Q-10, S-5
wrote, rote I-8
wry, rye M-7

your, you're A-1, C-5, E-2, F-5, H-4, I-1,
    J-7, K-1, K-3, L-2, O-2, W-3, W-6,
    W-9, W-10, X-7

ABOUT THE AUTHOR

William Strong teaches courses in writing, English methods, and secondary reading at Utah State University in Logan. He has also taught high school English in Portland, Oregon, and worked as a language arts consultant in eastern Idaho. His educational background includes bachelor's and master's degrees from Portland State College and the University of Oregon respectively; he was a TTT fellow at the University of Illinois, where he received a Ph.D. in English. In addition to journal publications, he authored *Sentence Combining: A Composing Book* (Random House, 1973, 1983), *Sentence Combining and Paragraph Building* (Random House, 1981), and co-authored *Facing Value Decisions: Rationale-Building for Teachers* (Teacher's College Press, 1982). He has been a speaker and workshop leader at many state, regional, and national meetings and a consultant for several school districts. At present he directs the Utah Writing Project and edits the *Utah English Journal*.